D0945864

ON

DOSTOEVSKY

Susan Leigh Anderson
University of Connecticut

WADSWORTH

TM

THOMSON LEARNING

Australia • Canada • Mexico • Singapore • Spain
United Kingdom • United States

Printed in the United States of America
1 2 3 4 5 6 7 04 03 02 01 00

For permission to use material from this text, contact us:
Web: http://www.thomsonrights.com
Fax: 1-800-730-2215
Phone: 1-800-730-2214

For more information, contact:
Wadsworth/Thomson Learning, Inc.
10 Davis Drive
Belmont, CA 94002-3098
USA
http://www.wadsworth.com

ISBN: 0-534-58372-5

Contents

Preface

The Russian critic and poet Vyacheslav Ivanov (1866-1949) said of the characters in Fyodor Dostoevsky's novels:

> They do not retreat from us with the passage of time; they do not age; they refuse to withdraw into the ethereal regions of the muses, there to become objects of our alien and dispassionate contemplation....in dark and sleepless nights they knock at our doors, frequent our bedsides and in confidential whispers engage us in many a disquieting conversation.[1]

No one doubts that Dostoevsky was a great writer, but many will find it strange to classify him as a philosopher since, with the exception of his collection of essays *The Diary of a Writer*, he wrote only fiction. I shall argue in this book that, despite the fact that most philosophers have chosen to do philosophy using essay style, it is not only possible to do philosophy in a work of fiction, but that a great writer can sometimes do philosophy more effectively in a work of fiction. Dostoevsky in the nineteenth century, and Albert Camus[2] in the twentieth century, are two examples of extremely gifted writers who were able to do philosophy successfully in works of fiction.

There are three reasons why philosophers should read Dostoevsky's novels. First, he was preoccupied with philosophical issues — with answering philosophical questions and solving philosophical problems — which is why he can be classified as being a philosopher. Dostoevsky was concerned with answering two fundamental philosophical questions: (i) What is the human predicament? and (ii) Given the answer to (i), how then should we live our lives? The first question involves Dostoevsky in metaphysical speculation — about free will, the nature of the self, and the existence of God — and the second leads him into the areas of ethics and metaethics. The philosophical problem which concerned him, above all, was this: After establishing that the most important attribute human

---

[1] Vyacheslav Ivanov, *Freedom and the Tragic Life, A Study in Dostoevsky*, The Noonday Press, New York, 1959, p. 3.
[2] See, for instance, Camus' novels *The Stranger*, *The Plague*, and *The Fall*.

beings possess is that they are free, and then realizing the destructive possibilities of this freedom, he sought a restraining force which would be compatible with freedom. And, in attempting to solve this problem, Dostoevsky has given us, in his chapters "Rebellion" and "The Grand Inquisitor" from *The Brothers Karamazov*, probably the finest discussion of the Problem of Evil — the problem of reconciling the existence of an omnipotent, omniscient, and benevolent God with the existence of evil in the world — that has ever been given. At least one of these chapters is invariably included in philosophical anthologies which discuss this classic problem.

Second, Dostoevsky is important to philosophy because of the influence he had upon, and affinity with, other philosophers. His work is generally considered to be, if not itself existentialist, then at least a precursor to Existentialism. Walter Kaufmann called Dostoevsky's *Notes From Underground* "the best overture for existentialism ever written."[1] Dostoevsky's emphasis on freedom, the anxiety this causes, and his attempt to integrate philosophy with real life certainly align him with later existentialists. Friedrich Nietzsche also found an affinity with Dostoevsky. He read *Notes from Underground,* in a French translation in December 1886, and wrote:

> I did not even know the name of Dostoevsky just a few weeks ago....An accidental reach of the arm in a bookstore brought to my attention *L'esprit souterrain*, a work just translated into French....The instinct of kinship (or how should I name it?) spoke up immediately; my joy was extraordinary.[2]

After reading this work of Dostoevsky's, Nietzsche had only two lucid years left; but it seems clear to a number of scholars that "the influence of the Russian was significant, perhaps even more significant than Nietzsche himself either recognized or was willing to admit."[3] In

---

[1] Walter Kaufmann, *Existentialism from Dostoevsky to Sartre*, The World Publishing Company, New York, 1964, p. 14.

[2] Quoted in Kaufmann, *Op. Cit.*, p. 52.

[3] Eric Luft and Douglas Stenberg, "Dostoevskii's Specific Influence on Nietzsche's Preface to *Daybreak*," *The Journal of the History of Ideas*, 1991, p. 442. See also C. A. Miller, "Nietzsche's 'Discovery' of Dostoevsky," *Nietzsche-Studien*, Vol. 2, 1973. Miller states that Nietzsche went on to read at least three, and possibly as many as five, other novels of Dostoevsky's; and that we can see the influence of

particular, we can see Dostoevsky's influence on the Preface to Nietzsche's *Daybreak*:

> What sets it apart from [Nietzsche's] other work...is its tone, its images, and its style, much of which can be traced to Dostoevskii. The preface reads as if Nietzsche had all of a sudden discovered in Dostoevskii a new way to say more clearly, more forcefully, and more dramatically the same things he had been saying for years.[1]

Finally, Dostoevsky's novels contain important criticisms of cherished views in philosophy and religion.[2] Dostoevsky questions the unity of the self, the rational defensibility of belief in God, the defense of morality based on reason, even the value of rationality itself![3] Yet Dostoevsky is not just a critic. It is easy to criticize everyone else's views, yet not offer anything else in their place. Dostoevsky does have a positive philosophy to offer us, a view of how we can make the most of our circumstances and lead freely chosen, happy lives, individually and collectively.

Whether we agree with his final position or not, we cannot doubt that Dostoevsky attained a level of understanding of human beings few have reached, partly because, as we shall see when we look at his life, of his own extraordinary life experiences. He thought deeply about the various possibilities for giving meaning to our lives. Ivanov says of Dostoevsky:

> At every palpitation of our hearts, he says to us: "Yes, I know; and I know more, and much else besides."...inexorably he stands before us, with his penetrating, enigmatic gaze, the sombre and keen-eyed guide through the labyrinth of our souls, simultaneously guiding us and spying upon us....He has asked the coming age questions that had never been asked before, and has whispered answers to questions not foreseen.[4]

Dostoevsky's work on *The Genealogy of Morals* (1887) as well.

[1] Luft and Stenberg, *Op. Cit.*, p. 460.

[2] This, I am sure, endeared him to Nietzsche.

[3] Since Dostoevsky did not believe that one could attain the truth through reason, through the intellect, it is understandable that he rejected conventional mediums for doing philosophy.

[4] Ivanov, *Op. Cit.*, pp. 3-4.

In this brief introduction to Dostoevsky's philosophy, I shall begin with a chapter on the question of whether, and to what extent, one can successfully do philosophy in a work of fiction. Then, after giving an account of Dostoevsky's life, I shall consider the development of his philosophy in the novels *The Double* (1846), *Notes from Underground* (1864), *Crime and Punishment* (1866), *The Idiot* (1869), *The Devils* (also translated as *The Possessed*) (1871-2), and his magnum opus *The Brothers Karamazov* (1879-80), after which I shall give a final assessment of Dostoevsky's overall philosophy.

It is important to note that I will not be giving a literary analysis of Dostoevsky's work. Thus, for example, in my discussion of the early novel *The Double*, I shall not be concerned with possible stylistic defects, problems with the plot, or other structural problems. Nor shall I comment on the historical events and attitudes which Dostoevsky was, in part, reacting to in his novels. I shall be concerned only with the philosophical position which he gradually develops and which is most fully presented in *The Bothers Karamazov*.

I am grateful to the University of Connecticut for allowing me to teach "Philosophy and Literature" for over twenty years, which has helped to prepare me for writing this book, and I would like to thank Yakira Frank and Kathy Brady for their generous editorial assistance in the preparation of the manuscript.

1

Philosophy and Fiction

"You have touched upon the very essence of the matter; by one stroke you have indicated the main thing....we try to explain this with words, but you, an artist, with one trait, with one stroke, in an image, you set forth the very gist, so that one can feel it with one's own hand, so as to enable the least reasoning reader to grasp everything at once! This is the mystery of art! This is the truth of art! This is the artist's service to truth!" (The critic V. G. Bielinsky, after reading Dostoevsky's first novel *Poor Folk*[1])

A few important historical philosophers — Plato, Hume, and Berkeley, for instance — wrote dialogues, and two nineteenth century philosophers — Friedrich Nietzsche and Søren Kierkegaard — experimented with other non-traditional modes of expressing philosophical theses;[2] but, for the most part, philosophers have largely

---

[1] Quoted in Fyodor Dostoevsky, *The Diary of a Writer*, excerpt from 1877, translated by Boris Brasol, George Braziller, New York, 1954, p. 587.

[2] Consider, in addition to Plato's numerous dialogues, Hume's *Dialogues Concerning Natural Religion*, Berkeley's *Three Dialogues Between Hylas and Philonous*, Nietzsche's *Thus Spoke Zarathustra* and

written using essay style. There is a feeling, among the majority of philosophers, that philosophy is one thing and fiction something else.[1] They have trouble thinking of those whose most famous works belong in the category of fiction as philosophers.

In the twentieth century, Jean-Paul Sartre wrote numerous plays and novels, but he also wrote traditional philosophical treatises which are probably better known, and this is why no one doubts that he was a philosopher. Albert Camus and Ayn Rand, on the other hand, who were clearly interested in philosophical questions, are not considered to be philosophers by many people because the work they are most known for is their fiction. But at least they also wrote essays to explain the philosophy in their novels. In the case of the nineteenth century writer Fyodor Dostoevsky, all his work, with the exception of *The Diary of a Writer*, was fiction, so it becomes even more difficult to think of him as a philosopher.

The bias against combining philosophy and fiction comes from the analytic movement which dominated twentieth century Anglo-American philosophical thought. According to the analytic method, one must express one's views as clearly as possible, in an unemotional fashion, defending them with arguments, defining crucial terms, and considering all possible objections to one's views. A work of fiction doesn't seem to be the ideal medium though which to accomplish this.

It is important, therefore, to begin our study of Dostoevsky's philosophy by asking the following questions: Can anything worthwhile philosophically be accomplished in a work of fiction? If so, are there limitations as to what can be done philosophically in a work of fiction? Can one ever do philosophy *as well* through the medium of fiction as it can be done in the traditional medium? Could it ever be done *better* in a work of fiction?

There are two general arguments which might be given to show that doing philosophy and writing fiction are essentially incompatible activities: First, it might be argued that fiction is, by definition, untrue; and since philosophy is concerned with the truth, philosophers cannot be fiction writers and fiction writers cannot be philosophers. Second, it can be maintained that philosophers must be clear, whereas fiction is best when ambiguous (that is, when different interpretations are

---

Kierkegaard's *Either/Or.*

[1] Many of the ideas which I present in this chapter first appeared in my article "Philosophy and Fiction," in *Metaphilosophy*, Vol. 23, No. 3, 1992.

possible); so, again, doing philosophy and writing fiction are essentially incompatible.

Looking at the first argument, it is important to ask in what sense fiction is untrue. Certainly fiction does not report the actions of actual beings. But to be successful, the characters must be believable and the actions they engage in must be possible. Furthermore, all serious works of fiction must have a point to make — English teachers call it the "theme" of the story — which we should recognize as giving us some sort of "truth" about life.

The second argument seems to be much stronger, and I think it does point out a major difference between the styles of the typical philosopher and the typical fiction writer. Philosophers generally want to make a point or series of points as *directly* and *clearly* as possible. They would be upset to learn that their readers are not sure exactly what they are saying. Fiction writers, on the other hand, are usually not upset if their stories are interpreted differently by different readers, even if some of those interpretations were unintended. And with their intended themes, they are admonished to "show, not tell." The communication of a message should be done *indirectly*.

Philosophers have generally opted for the direct communication of essay-style writing over the indirect communication of fiction writing. Essay-style writing was particularly suited to the extremely specialized work of most twentieth century philosophers and their lack of talent for, and interest in, writing fiction; but for some types of work in philosophy, the indirect communication of a skilled fiction-writer may make sense and even be preferable.

The desired ambiguity in a work of fiction is not incompatible with clarity and consistency. The multiple layers of meaning which are possible in a work of fiction can each be quite clear and consistent with one another. Thus Camus' novel *The Plague* can be both a commentary on the Second World War and more generally about how one should react to the essential condition of life's being "absurd"[1]. Similarly, Isaac Asimov's short story "The Bicentennial Man" can simultaneously be a story about American history and about what criterion should be used to determine whether a being has moral rights.

The main argument that can be given in favor of expressing philosophical ideas through fiction is this: If philosophy is supposed to

---

[1] Basically what Camus meant by the "absurd" is the conjunction of the facts that life has no meaning in and of itself and yet human beings insist on giving it a meaning.

be relevant to life, as at least the "big" philosophical issues are supposed to be, then why not present it in a lifelike situation, through the characters in a play, novel, or short story? The existentialist idea that philosophy should not be a detached academic endeavor, but rather should be integrated with life,[1] can be used to support the main premise of this argument. Thus Sartre maintained:

> [Though] the problems which the present age poses can be treated abstractly by philosophical reflection...we whose purpose it is to live those problems [must] sustain our thinking by those imaginative and concrete experiences which are novels.[2]

And, according to Camus, "a novel is never anything but a philosophy put into fiction."[3] Barbara Brandon states that Ayn Rand wrote fiction because:

> She wanted an activity that...would unite theory and its practical application. That desire was an essential element in the continuing appeal that fiction held for her: fiction made possible the integration of wide abstract principles and their direct expression in and application to man's life. She wanted to define a moral ideal,...and to project, through fiction, the living reality of that ideal.[4]

There are three further reasons why it might be a good idea to combine philosophy with fiction: First, fiction allows us to experience perspectives which are unlike our own, as we enter into the minds of characters who do not think in the way we do or who have very different basic beliefs, and it also allows us to experience what it might

---

[1] According to Kaufmann, "a marked dissatisfaction with traditional philosophy as superficial, academic, and remote from life" is one of the main characteristics of Existentialism. See Kaufmann, *Op. Cit.*, p. 12.
[2] Quoted in Robert Cumming, "The Literature of Extreme Situations," in *Aesthetics Today*, edited by Morris Philipson, The World Publishing Company, 1964, p. 403.
[3] Quoted in *Writers on Writing*, edited by Jon Winokur, Running Press, Philadelphia, 1986, p. 38.
[4] Barbara Brandon, *The Passion of Ayn Rand*, Doubleday, New York, 1986.

be like to live in circumstances very different from our own. A skilled writer, with an important point to make, can use this effectively to give readers an insight into an issue which might be hard to accept in a theoretical discussion of the issue.

Second, just because the communicating of a thesis in a good work of fiction is done indirectly, readers must actively participate in the reasoning process. They must draw the proper conclusion themselves, and the result is that they are more likely to take the thesis to heart. Janet Burroway, in her book *Writing Fiction*, nicely characterizes this feature of a work of fiction. She says that since the author "let[s] us use our senses and do our own generalizing and interpreting, we will be involved as participants in a real way."[1] Somewhat paradoxically, one can even say that skillful indirect presentation of a thesis in a work of fiction can communicate that thesis more directly, by affecting us in an immediate way rather than via the intellect. This explains Bielinsky's assertion that Dostoevsky could, as "an artist, with one trait, with one stroke, in an image,...set forth the very gist, so that one can feel it with one's own hand, so as to enable the least reasoning reader to grasp everything at once!"

This leads us to the last reason why it can be a good idea to combine philosophy with fiction. The emotional impact of a good work of fiction is likely to be greater than a conventional philosophical work; so, although both may raise an important question, the work of fiction is more likely to make us *care* about answering it. For instance, no philosopher writing in the usual essay style has made us feel the weight of the problem of evil as much as Dostoevsky in *The Brothers Karamazov* or Camus in *The Plague*.

Even analytic philosophers have found it helpful to use fiction to a limited extent in their work. Some have introduced a story to provide a counterexample to refute a commonly accepted view: "Most people believe such and such, but think about this case...." A well known example is Judith Jarvis Thomson's violinist analogy to refute the anti-abortion argument that if the fetus a person, then it must necessarily be wrong to end its life.[2] Others have used a story to convince the reader that a controversial position is defensible. Jonathan Bennett, for instance, used Mark Twain's *The Adventures of*

---

[1] Janet Burroway, *Writing Fiction*, Second Edition, Little, Brown and Company, Boston, 1987, p. 80.

[2] See Judith Jarvis Thomson, "A Defense of Abortion," *Philosophy and Public Affairs*, vol. I, no. 1, 1971.

Huckleberry Finn to convince us that when someone is in a moral temptation situation, it is possible for us to wish that he would do what he is *inclined* to do, rather than what he thinks he *should* do.[1] Analytic philosophers have also used stories to illustrate something which is very difficult to express. Antony Flew, R. M. Hare and Basil Mitchell, for instance, all gave parables to characterize their views of the nature of religious belief in a symposium on "Theology and Falsification."[2] And some analytic philosophers have used stories and dialogues to explore philosophical issues in order to make them more accessible to students and laypersons. Good examples are John Perry's *A Dialogue on Personal Identity and Immortality* and *Dialogue on Good, Evil, and the Existence of God* as well as Wesley Salmon's "An Encounter with David Hume."[3]

There is no limit to what one can do philosophically in a work of fiction, as long as the philosophical issues raised are ones which affect our own, or possible beings', lives. Recently, some of the most philosophical fiction has been found in science fiction literature,[4] and this literature demonstrates the wide range of issues which can be tackled in a work of fiction. Robert Sheckley's story "Seventh Victim" raises the questions of whether there are limits as to what consenting adults should be permitted to do, and whether the right thing to do is that which results in the best consequences. Robert Heinlein's story "All You Zombies —" attempts to demonstrate that time travel can be intelligible.[5] Philip Dick's "Imposter" convinces us, essentially because

---

[1] See Jonathan Bennett, "The Conscience of Huckleberry Finn," *Philosophy*, Vol. 49, 1974.

[2] In *New Essays in Philosophical Theology*, edited by Antony Flew and Alasdair MacIntyre, Macmillan, New York, 1955.

[3] John Perry, *A Dialogue on Personal Identity and Immortality* and *Dialogue on Good, Evil, and the Existence of God*, Hackett Publishing Co., Inc., Indianapolis, 1978 and 1999 respectively. Wesley Salmon, "An Encounter with David Hume," in *Reason and Responsibility*, Third Edition, edited by Joel Feinberg, Wadsworth Publishing Co., Belmont, CA, 1975.

[4] The stories I mention as examples, as well as many others, can be found in *Philosophy and Science Fiction*, edited by Michael Philips, Prometheus Books, Buffalo, N. Y., 1984.

[5] David Lewis believes he is successful. See David Lewis, "The Paradoxes of Time Travel," *American Philosophical Quarterly*, Vol. 13, 1976.

of the problem of distinguishing between real and apparent memory, that an individual himself may not be in the best position to know who he is. Heinlein's "They" considers epistemological questions, including the problem of other minds. E. M. Forster's "The Machine Stops" explores the ramifications of a world which has become totally dependent upon technology. Isaac Asimov's story "The Bicentennial Man" raises issues like the following: What is a person? Is it conceivable that a machine, a robot, could think? have feelings? And, as I mentioned earlier, what criterion should be used to determine whether a being has moral rights?

I shall mention two other examples of particularly ambitious twentieth century philosophical works of fiction: John Barth's short story "Night-Sea Journey," from *Lost in the Funhouse*, considers, through the thoughts of a sperm on its way to being united with an egg, different ways of trying to justify our existence. What is life all about? How should we live it? Barth gives us the standard responses to these questions and criticizes them. Last, but not least, Sartre manages to present us with his entire philosophy in his novel *The Age of Reason*. We are shown that our essence is freedom, what this entails, models of people living in bad faith and those living authentically, and how one could become paralyzed to act by the realization that one is free. The novel also demonstrates that we are social beings. Others' opinions of us determine to a large extent how we see ourselves; and others tend to label us, which we usually resent because we know that we are free, that we can't be labeled until we die.

I am convinced that a work of fiction can be highly philosophical, and I believe that philosophical fiction can have a greater impact on the reader than a conventional philosophical work. I think, however, that there are very few examples of really *great* philosophical fiction. One must have a true talent for writing fiction to pull it off successfully. There is always the danger that, in the hands of a less skilled writer, that the philosophical theses will overpower the fiction. The more philosophy one attempts to explicitly pack into a work of fiction, the less likely that the results will be good fiction. It will read like the work of a philosopher who tried to combine philosophy with fiction, rather than the work of a talented fiction writer who happens also to be a philosopher. Dostoevsky is one of the best examples of a great writer who happened also to be a philosopher.

2

Dostoevsky's Life

Fyodor Mikhail Dostoevsky was born in Moscow on October 30, 1821, the second of a physician's seven children. His father, Mikhail Andreevich Dostoevsky had been called up by the army, while studying at the Academy of Medicine and Surgery, just before the Battle of Borodino in 1812. He worked in overcrowded, foul-smelling, rear-line army hospitals for many years — performing numerous operations, including amputations — before he was discharged from the military in December of 1820, with the rank of medical officer first class. He was only thirty at the time, but he had lost all zest for living as the result of his experiences dealing with the victims of war.

In March of 1821, the doctor was appointed to a post at the Mariinskaya Hospital for the Poor, an architecturally magnificent structure situated in one of the most squalid neighborhoods in Moscow. He and his wife, Maria Fyodorovna Nechaeva, whom he had married in 1819, moved into an apartment provided by the hospital with their first-born son, Mikhail. Six months later Fyodor Mikhail was born. Six more children were born to the couple (one lived only a few days) before Maria Dostoevsky died, at the age of only thirty-seven, worn out by repeated pregnancies and ravaged by tuberculosis.

Dostoevsky's father — said to be a faithful husband, responsible father, and believing Christian; but also a suspicious, miserly, alcoholic man, with an uncontrollable temper, who grimly did his duty in life — came from an old noble family. In the eighteenth century, when the

8

family refused to accept Roman Catholicism in place of Russian Orthodoxy, they were excluded from the ranks of western nobility and became impoverished.

The atmosphere of Dostoevsky's boyhood home was oppressive and joyless, relieved only by the presence of his loving and creative mother, the wonderful fairy tales told by a succession of wet-nurses brought in from a near-by village, visits with an aunt, and his friendship with his older brother Mikhail, who later became Dostoevsky's closest friend and collaborator.

Dostoevsky's mother came from humble folk — artisans and tradespeople — but her own mother, Dostoevsky's maternal grandmother, came from the *Raznochintsy*, as educated members of the poorer classes were called in the eighteenth century. Dostoevsky's mother was fond of poetry, an avid reader of novels, very musical, and had a talent for writing beautiful and vivid letters. She was the first teacher of her children.

The wet-nurses employed by the Dostoevskys, who were from the class of serfs and therefore without rights, awakened Dostoevsky's interest, through the tales they told, in the emotionally charged and highly expressive oral poetry of the simple Russian people. This would bear fruit in his later writings.

Dostoevsky's mother's older sister, Alexandra Kumanina, married a member of Moscow's merchant aristocracy. Through her, Dostoevsky was exposed to the values of the merchant class: that money was equivalent to power, and that one should be devoted to the church and loyal to the Tsar. Dostoevsky undoubtedly noticed the difference between the Kumanins' way of life — they lived in an ornate house, filled with expensive art objects, situated on a bluff overlooking a river — and his own family's modest circumstances, as well as the poverty of the patients whom he met in the hospital gardens.

A variety of books filled the Dostoevsky's family bookcase and fed Fyodor's growing interest in literature: The Bible, the "Gothic" novels of the pioneering eighteenth century author Ann Radcliffe, Karamzin's twelve-volume *History of the Russian State*, the poetry of Pushkin, Lermontov and Schiller, and the novels of Sir Walter Scott and Nikolay Gogol, among others.

In 1827, Dostoevsky's father was promoted to the higher civil service rank of collegiate assessor, the equivalent of Major in the army, a rank that carried with it hereditary gentility and the right to own land with serfs. In 1831, when Dostoevsky was ten years old, his father purchased the village of Darovoe, about seventy-five miles southeast of

Moscow, and the following year he purchased the adjacent hamlet of Cheremoshna. Thus, the Dostoevskys acquired an estate of about fourteen hundred acres of land and one hundred serfs. The land had no rivers or forests, the soil was poor, the manor house was a tiny mud-walled structure, and the serfs were extremely poor and backward. It was on this dreary estate that Dostoevsky spent his school holidays.

Dostoevsky's father and mother differed in their attitudes towards their newly acquired serfs. Whereas the father abused his power over them, frequently whipping them, with the result that the peasants hated him and hoped one day to get their revenge,[1] his mother treated them leniently and with compassion. From her, Dostoevsky learned sympathy and pity for the downtrodden.

Dostoevsky was aware of another example of a "friend of the downtrodden," Fyodor Petrovich Haas, who was appointed city physician of Moscow in the mid-1820s and then, in 1828, head physician of Moscow's prisons. Haas succeeded in introducing a number of humane reforms into the punitive system, accompanied many convicts far along the road to Siberia, and provided them with clothing and money, dying a revered pauper himself in 1853. He was probably Dostoevsky's first model of an ideal person; he appeared briefly as a character in *The Idiot*.

Dr. Dostoevsky personally taught his sons Latin, forcing them to remain standing during lessons. Later they were taught French by a Monsieur Souchard, who also ran a preparatory day school which he convinced Dr. Dostoevsky that the two older boys should attend. Thus, in January 1933, Mikhail and Fyodor began attending the Drachusov School. The caste-like atmosphere, with brutal initiation rites, was very disturbing to Dostoevsky. He later wrote about it in his semi-autobiographical novel *A Raw Youth*.

In the autumn of 1834 the brothers were transferred to Leopold Chermak's boarding school. The staff included many eminent Moscow teachers and scholars, and the emphasis of the school was on literature. One of Dostoevsky's classmates described the future writer at this time in his life:

> He was a serious, thoughtful boy with blond hair and a pale face. He was not much interested in games. During breaks he

---

[1] We should note that, in *The Brothers Karamazov*, Cheremoshna is mentioned as being in the possession of the dissolute and cruel father Fyodor Karamazov.

hardly ever left his books, and when he did, it was to talk with the older pupils.[1]

During the time he was at the Chermak school — a time of Russian literary upheaval, as Pushkin was killed in a duel, Lermontov was exiled to the Caucasus, and Gogol went abroad "with a melancholy heart"[2] — Dostoevsky began to be aware of his calling. He said later that when he was about fifteen, he felt the first stirrings of inspiration: *"There was a kind of fire in my soul, and I believed in it*; as for what would come of it, I did not much care."[3]

After the birth of her last child, in July 1835, Dostoevsky's mother's tuberculosis worsened. By the beginning of 1837, she never left her small darkened bedroom. She died on February 27th. Her death devastated the Dostoevsky family. The Kumanins took two of the children to raise and financially helped the others as well. Mikhail and Fyodor were taken by their father to St. Petersburg where Fyodor was enrolled in the Military Engineering Academy, located in the massive Mikhailovsky Palace where Tsar Paul I had been assassinated in 1801, and Mikhail, who was rejected by the Academy due to problems with his lungs, was enrolled in the Engineering Cadets and subsequently assigned to the Engineering Command in the Baltic seaport of Reval.

En route to the capital, Fyodor witnessed a scene which was to haunt him for the rest of his life and which later served as the inspiration for a passage in *Crime and Punishment*[4]:

> One evening we were stopping at a station, an inn, in some village....It was a large and well-to-do village. In half an hour we were to resume our journey and, meanwhile, I was looking through the window, and I saw the following:
>
> Across the street, directly opposite the inn, was the station building. Suddenly a courier's troika speedily drove up to the station's platform; a courier jumped out of the carriage....The courier was a tall, very stout and strong chap, with a livid face.

---

[1] Quoted in Leonid Grossman, *Dostoevsky, A Biography*, translated by Mary Mackler, The Bobbs-Merrill Company, New York, 1975, p. 19.

[2] See Grossman, *Op. Cit.*, p. 19.

[3] Quoted in Grossman, *Op. Cit.*, p. 19.

[4] Raskolnikov's dream about a tormented peasant nag, dying as its frenzied master beat it with a crowbar.

He ran into the station house and there, surely, must have "swallowed" a glass of vodka....

Meanwhile, a fresh, spirited, substitute troika drove up to the postal station, and the yamschik, a young lad of about twenty, in a red shirt and holding an overcoat in his hands, jumped into the coachman's seat. Forthwith, the courier came running down the staircase and seated himself in the carriage. The yamschik stirred on, but hardly had he started to move than the courier rose up and silently raised his hardy right fist and, from above, painfully brought it down on the back of the yamschik's head. He jolted forward, lifted his whip and, with all his strength, lashed the wheel horse....the dreadful fist soared again and again and struck blows on the back of the head. And then, again and again, and thus it continued until the troika disappeared out of sight. Of course, the yamschik, who could hardly keep his balance, incessantly, every second, like a madman, lashed the horses and, finally, he had whipped them up to the point where they started dashing at top speed, as if possessed.[1]

Dr. Dostoevsky wanted his sons to have successful careers in military engineering, which was considered to be an extremely profitable field at the time, since large numbers of fortresses were being built on the western frontier of the country. Fyodor, however, had no aptitude for military engineering. He was a conscientious student; but his favorite subjects were literature, history, drawing and architecture. While at the Engineering Academy, he cherished the time he had in the evenings when he could write down "his early reflections on the enormous theme that possessed him: 'Man is a mystery that must be divined!'"[2] He also enjoyed conversing with Ivan Nikolaevich Shidlovsky, the first in a series of philosopher friends, a man five years his senior whom the Dostoevskys first met in a hotel when they arrived in St. Petersburg.

Meanwhile, after Dr. Dostoevsky left his sons in St. Petersburg, he returned to Moscow and resigned his hospital post, pleading poor health. He retired to his estate, accompanied by a former servant, who became his mistress, and his younger children. He drank very heavily, let himself deteriorate and, on June 8, 1839, was apparently murdered

---

[1] *The Diary of a Writer*, 1876, *Op. Cit.*, p. 185.
[2] Grossman, *Op. Cit.*, p. 29.

by his own serfs, after continuing to abuse them. The Kumanins assumed responsibility for the remaining younger Dostoevsky children. When the news of his father's death reached Fyodor, he had his first serious attack of convulsions and fainting, a condition which was much later diagnosed as epilepsy. He was clearly troubled by his own feelings towards his father and the circumstances surrounding his death. According to his daughter:

> All his life long he analysed the reasons for that horrible death. When he was working on the characterization of Fyodor Karamazov, perhaps he recalled his father's miserliness, which caused his sons so much suffering and angered them so, and his drunkenness and the physical revulsion he inspired in his children.[1]

After completing the first three years of the Academy's curriculum, Fyodor was permitted, in 1840, to move into a small, dark, two-room apartment with a fellow student. Income received from a brother-in-law, who became the custodian of Dr. Dostoevsky's estate and the legal guardian of his two older sons, supplemented Fyodor's pay as an officer and allowed him to lead an active social life. However, Dostoevsky frequently found himself short of money, due to his reckless generosity. This was a problem that plagued him all his life. It was, perhaps, a reaction against his father's stinginess and also arose from his having had little experience managing finances. He began a vicious cycle of borrowing and spending, and later developed a passion for gambling to try to pay his debts. It seemed to be a part of his temperament to live life impulsively and passionately, close to the edge, as he admitted later in his life: "Everywhere and in everything I go to the limit. All my life I have crossed the last line."[2]

In 1840-41, Dostoevsky worked on two historical dramas, *Maria Stuart* and *Boris Godunov*, which have not survived. Granted a month's leave of absence in the summer of 1842, Dostoevsky used the time to visit his brother Mikhail and his new German wife. Dostoevsky graduated from the Engineering Academy on August 12, 1843, following which he was assigned to the drafting department of the St. Petersburg Engineering Command. This desk assignment was tedious and unpleasant for "the strong, ardent soul of one who cannot bear his

---

[1] Quoted in Grossman, *Op. Cit.*, p. 42

[2] Quoted in Grossman, *Op. Cit.*, p. 49.

banal daily schedule and calendar of life," he wrote in a letter.[1] Dostoevsky continued to lead a rather wild social life, digging himself deeper into debt. By December of 1843, his financial situation was so bad that he imprudently renounced any claim to his father's estate in exchange for a small lump sum from his brother-in-law. In a further attempt to augment his income, he translated Balzac's *Eugénie Grandet*, which was published in the June and July 1844 issues of the journal *Repetoire and Pantheon*.

In the year of his first publication, Dostoevsky was ordered to take an extended trip to a distant fortress, which would have taken him away from his writing for several months. He made the decision to hand in his resignation and devote himself entirely to his literary vocation. On October 19, 1844 he was discharged from the service with the rank of lieutenant.

Dostoevsky began working on his first novel, *Poor Folk*, a "social" novel which also contained important psychological insights. He said later that he "wrote the novel passionately, almost with tears." When he finished *Poor Folk* in May of 1845, he gave the manuscript to a friend, the writer Dmitry Vasilievich Grigorovich, who in turn took it to show Nikolay Alexeevich Nekrasov, a radical poet, journalist and publisher. The two of them sat up all night, taking turns reading *Poor Folk* to each other. The next day, Nekrasov took it to the celebrated critic Vissarion Grigorievich Bielinsky, telling him that "a new Gogol has appeared!" Bielinksy was skeptical, remarking to Nekrasov that "Gogols grow like mushrooms in your midst!" But after reading the novel, Bielinsky too was enthralled. Dostoevsky recorded, in *The Diary of a Writer,* that when he was brought to the critic:

> [Bielinsky] began to speak ardently with burning eyes. "But do you, yourself, understand" he repeated to me several times, screaming, as was his habit — "what you have written!".... "To you, as an artist, truth is revealed and declared; it came to you as a gift. Treasure, then, your gift, be faithful to it, and you will become a great writer!"[2]

Dostoevsky never forgot Bielinsky's words. Hearing them was a turning point in his life:

---

[1] Quoted in Alba Amoia, *Feodor Dostoevsky*, Continuum Publishing Company, New York, 1993, p. 25.

[2] *The Diary of a Writer, Op. Cit.*, p. 587.

I felt that a solemn moment had occurred in my life, a break forever; that something altogether new had begun, something I had not anticipated even in my most impassioned dreams. (And in those days I was an awful dreamer.) "And am I in truth so great?" — I was bashfully asking myself in a state of timid ecstacy....I shall earn this praise!....This was the most delightful minute in my whole life.[1]

In January of 1846, *Poor Folk* was published in Nekrasov's *Petersburg Miscellany*. Dostoevsky's second novel *The Double* appeared in early February in *Notes of the Fatherland*, the leading progressive journal of the time. Reviewers were not impressed with either work, and even Bielinsky was lukewarm in his reaction to *The Double*. According to Alba Amoia, "at bottom, Bielinsky's didactic, socialistic, and realistic conceptions of literature were sharply at variance with Dostoevsky's more romantic and idealistic approach."[2]

Before Dostoevsky and Bielinsky broke off relations completely in 1847 — in part because Dostoevsky was disturbed by Bielinsky's atheism — Dostoevsky enjoyed socializing with the Bielinsky circle. He was invited to the home of Ivan Ivanovich Panaev, a fashionable fiction writer of the 1840's. Here he experienced love for the first time: "Yesterday I was at Panaev's for the first time, and I seem to have fallen in love with his wife."[3] Panaev's beautiful and intelligent wife was unhappily married. She loved life and was unusually kind and sympathetic when others began ridiculing Dostoevsky. His infatuation with her was brief, but important in his life. She was very likely the inspiration for Nastasya Filippovna in *The Idiot*.

Always needing money, Dostoevsky quickly wrote *Mr. Prokharchin*, *The Landlady* and several short stories, mostly published in *Notes of the Fatherland*. He complained to his brother:

> When will I get out of debt? It's a bad thing to work as a day laborer. You'll destroy everything, including talent and youth and hope, grow disgusted with your work, and in the end become a pen pusher, not a writer.[4]

---

[1] *The Diary of a Writer*, pp. 587-8.

[2] Amoia, *Op. Cit.*, p. 29.

[3] Quoted, from his *Letters*, in Amoia, *Op. Cit.*, p. 28.

[4] *Ibid.*, p. 29.

Still, Dostoevsky was hopeful that his next novel, *Netochka Nezvanova*, on which he worked for a year, would be received with critical acclaim and ensure his financial recovery. The first two parts were published in the January and February issues of *Notes of the Fatherland* in 1849. The third part did not appear until May of that year, and without Dostoevsky's name. He had been arrested on April 23, 1849 and imprisoned for suspicion of revolutionary activity.

As early as the spring of 1846, Dostoevsky had become acquainted with Mikhail Vasilievich Butashevich-Petrashevsky, a disciple of the French social philosopher Charles Fourier, and the leader of a reading and discussion group in St. Petersburg that was known as the Petrashevsky circle. In the spring of 1847, Dostoevsky began attending meetings of the circle, at which diverse opinions on contemporary events and socio-economic problems were discussed. He was attracted to Fourierism for its "love of humanity," and he thought it was possible to achieve their shared utopian dream through the printed and spoken word. Dostoevsky was never in sympathy with violent revolution to bring about a better society.

Nevertheless, by the spring of 1849, the Tsarist government, having become alarmed by the occurrence of revolutionary violence in several European countries, decided to put an end to the activities of the Petrashevsky circle and Dostoevsky, together with thirty-three other members of the circle and a satellite group, was arrested. Dostoevsky's brother was also arrested a few days later. Mikhail, who had retired from government service by this time and settled in St. Petersburg with his family, had also joined the Petrashevsky circle. He was released soon after his arrest, but Dostoevsky was imprisoned in the formidable Peter and Paul Fortress and put into solitary confinement during the investigation, which took four months. A trial, lasting a month and a half, followed. Dostoevsky, and fourteen others, were sentenced to death by firing squad.

Although Tsar Nicolas I changed the sentence, three days later, to four years of hard labor in Siberia to be followed by years of service as a common soldier, the prisoners were not told of this. For over a month, they awaited their death. On the instructions of the Tsar, all the preparations for execution on December 22, 1849 were carried out and, just before firing, the prisoners were finally told that their lives had been spared.[1] To have come so close to death surely changed

---

[1] Dostoevsky put his near-execution ordeal into *The Idiot*, in Prince Myshkin's story about a political prisoner he had known.

Dostoevsky's life forever. Despite the ordeal which still lay ahead of him, Dostoevsky wrote to Mikhail the night that his life was spared:

> My brother, I do not feel despondent and have not lost heart. Life is everywhere. Life is in ourselves and not outside us. There will be men beside me, and the important thing is...whatever the misfortunes, not to despair and not to fall — that is the aim of life, that is its purpose. I realize this now. The idea has entered into my flesh and my blood....Life is a gift; life is happiness, every minute of it could have been an eternity of happiness. Brother, I swear to you that I will not lose hope and will keep my spirit and my heart pure.[1]

Two days later, when he was permitted to have one last visit with Mikhail, he consoled his brother, maintaining that:

> I am not going to my grave. You are not seeing me into my coffin. They are not animals in prison, they are men, perhaps better men than I. And when I get out I'll start writing. I have been through a great deal during these months; within myself I have been through a great deal, and I expect I shall see and experience more — I'll have plenty to write about.[2]

The next day, on Christmas Eve, Dostoevsky and his fellow convicts set out in chains on the two-thousand mile journey to Tobolsk, in western Siberia. Upon reaching the transit prison at Tobolsk, Dostoevsky was then sent five hundred miles further up the Irtish River to the prison camp at Omsk. There he labored for four years with common thieves and murderers who had as much contempt for him, as an educated member of the nobility, as the guards. True to his words to his brother, he was able to find in this experience material for many of his later novels, particularly *House of the Dead* in which he said "it was only a passionate desire for resurrection, for renewal, for a new life" that kept him going through those terrible years. The hardest thing of all for him was not to be able to write, nor have books to read. He was permitted only a copy of the *New Testament* while at Omsk.

---

[1] Quote in Grossman, *Op. Cit.*, pp. 163-4.
[2] Reported by Alexander Milyukov, who was also present. Quoted in Grossman, *Op. Cit.*, p. 165.

At the end of January of 1854, Dostoevsky's chains were removed and he was sent to Semipalatinsk, a remote town not far from the Chinese border, to serve as a private in the Seventh Line Battalion of the Siberian Army Corps. Allowed to read and write again, Dostoevsky wrote his brother, requesting him to send a long list of books — including Kant's *Critique of Pure Reason* and Hegel's *History of Philosophy* — and he began working on *House of the Dead*.

While at Semipalatinsk, Dostoevsky became romantically attached to pretty and intelligent Maria Dmitrievna Isaev, the wife of a drunken customs official who had lost his job. When the Isaevs left Semipalatinsk, after her husband finally found another job in Kuznetsk, Dostoevsky was miserable. Maria's husband died in August 1855, leaving her destitute in a remote town, suffering from tuberculosis, and with a young son. Dostoevsky did all he could to help her. When she considered marrying a young schoolteacher, Dostoevsky despaired that he might lose the woman who had come to mean so much to him. Partly to make himself a suitable candidate for marriage, he wrote to Eduard Totleben, a former acquaintance from his days at the Engineering Academy who had become an aide-de-camp of the Tsar, asking for his help in ending his indefinite sentence of serving as lowly private in the army. The new, more liberal, Tsar Alexander II decided to raise Dostoevsky's rank to the officer's status of ensign.

With his improved prospects, Maria agreed to marry him. The only obstacle was the money needed for the marriage ceremony and to set up housekeeping, which he managed to obtain from friends and disapproving relatives. They were married on February 6, 1957 in Kuznetsk. On the journey back to Semipalatinsk, Dostoevsky had an attack of "true epilepsy," diagnosed by a doctor, which frightened his wife and raised new concerns about Dostoevsky's future. On March 18, 1959 Dostoevsky received approval for a medical discharge from the service. He was pensioned with the rank of second lieutenant, but he was also placed under permanent police surveillance. After at first being denied permission to live in either Moscow or St. Petersburg, Dostoevsky was finally allowed to return to St. Petersburg in mid-December, ten years after his exile had begun.

Meanwhile, Dostoevsky had begun writing again. In 1959, two short stories were published; and in 1860, the first part of *House of the Dead* appeared in the newspaper *Russian World*. In 1862, the last part of *House of the Dead* appeared in *Time*, a new literary-political periodical which had been created by the Dostoevsky brothers in 1860, along with a reprinting of the first part. In between, Dostoevsky published *The Insulted and Injured*, a treatment of social injustice, in the first seven issues of *Time* in 1861.

Dostoevsky's marriage to Maria Dmitrievna turned out not to be very happy, although he would not divorce the woman who was already dying of consumption and whom, in his way, he still loved. In 1860, Dostoevsky became close to the talented stage actress Alexandra Shubert, who attracted him in part because her parents were serfs. This appealed to his growing conviction that "Russia's salvation lay in the soil and the [common] people."[1] In 1862, after returning from a disappointing summer trip to Europe,[2] Dostoevsky began a tempestuous relationship with the young feminist Apollinaria (Polina) Suslova, also the daughter of an emancipated serf, who at first idolized the celebrated writer who had suffered so much for his ideas. Soon, however, the relationship became a "love-hate" one which had mostly ended by the autumn of 1863, after Dostoevsky had followed Polina first to Paris and then to Italy and Germany. Still, it is believed that "Apollinaria Suslova was the strongest passion in Dostoevsky's life."[3] They had contact for many years afterwards, and Dostoevsky did propose to her after his wife died on April 15, 1864.

Dostoevsky's trip to Europe in 1863 provided the inspiration for a future novel, *The Gambler*. He gambled often on that trip. After one experience in Wiesbaden in September 1863, he wrote to his brother, following initial success with a "system" he had devised:

> Tell me, how could I help being carried away after this, how could I help believing that if I followed my system strictly I would have a fortune in my hands? And I need money so badly. For me, for you, for my wife, to write a novel. People win tens of thousands here without even trying. Yes, I went with the hope of saving us all and protecting myself from disaster.[4]

---

[1] See Grossman, *Op. Cit.*, p. 272.

[2] He wrote about this trip in *Winter Notes about Summer Impressions*, published in *Time* in 1863. On this trip, during a brief visit to London, Dostoevsky saw the "Crystal Palace" exhibition which became, for him, a metaphor for all that he detested in the materialistic civilization of the West. See, in particular, *Notes from Underground*.

[3] Grossman, *Op. Cit.*, p. 292.

[4] *Ibid.*, p. 296.

Meanwhile, the Tsar ordered that *Time* stop publication in May 1863, after a controversial article appeared in the journal concerning the recent Polish insurrection; but permission to start a new magazine, *Epoch*, was granted soon after. Dostoevsky's *Notes from Underground*, a novel in which he rejected the socialism which had attracted him in his youth, was published in the March and June 1864 issues.

Sadly, Dostoevsky's brother Mikhail died on July 10, 1864, just three months after Dostoevsky's wife's death, leaving him in despair, with Mikhail's widow and children looking to him "for salvation" and a magazine that was deeply in debt. To make matters worse, Dostoevsky's friend and colleague, Apollon Grigoryev, also died in September of that year.

With the threat of debtors' prison looming over him, Dostoevsky borrowed ten thousand roubles from his now elderly and senile aunt Alexandra Kumanina, but it still wasn't enough money. By the summer of 1865, *Epoch* ceased publication. Dostoevsky decided to go abroad where, away from creditors, he might be able to concentrate on his writing. But his situation became still worse as he lost all his money gambling in Wiesbaden.

At this point, while literally starving, Dostoevsky conceived the idea for one of his greatest novels, *Crime and Punishment*. He wrote to the editor of the *Russian Messenger*, Mikhail Nikiforovich Katkov, about his idea:

> It is a psychological account of a crime. The action is contemporary, this year. A young man of petit-bourgeois background has been expelled from the university and is living in extreme poverty. Lacking seriousness and stability in his mental makeup, he has given himself over to certain strange, 'half-baked' ideas in the air at the time, determines to escape from his vile situation at one stroke. He resolves to murder an old woman, widow of a titular councillor, who lends money for interest, and with that money to bring happiness to his mother, who lives in the provinces, and deliver his sister, who is employed as a companion in a landowner's family, from the threat of immanent ruin due to the lascivious attentions of the head of the house. He will then complete his studies, go abroad, and for the rest of his life be honest, steady and unswerving in fulfilment of his 'humane debt to mankind', whereby he will, of course, 'redress his crime', if, indeed, the word crime can be applied to his deed

20

against a deaf, stupid, evil, sick old woman who does not know herself what she lives for in the world and who might, perhaps, have died a natural death in a month's time....he succeeds by pure luck in doing the deed quickly and successfully....[But then] Unanswerable questions arise in the murderer's mind and unsuspected emotions torment his heart. The truth of God and the law of the earth take their toll and in the end he has an inner compulsion to go and confess....[1]

Katkov sent Dostoevsky an advance payment of three hundred roubles for the story, which saved him financially for the moment. He worked on the novel throughout the fall of 1865 and into the next year. *Crime and Punishment* appeared in the *Russian Messenger* throughout 1866.

Dostoevsky had also committed himself to a deadline of November 1, 1866 for his novel *The Gambler*, for which publisher Feodor Timofevich Stellovsky had advanced him money in the summer of 1865. By the beginning of October 1866, he had not written a single line. A friend suggested that he hire a secretary who knew shorthand and dictate the novel to her. In this way, on October 4, 1866, twenty-year-old Anna Grigoryevna Snitkina, who became his second wife, entered his life. Fifty years later she spoke of her first impression of Dostoevsky:

> No words can convey the depressing and pathetic impression Fyodor Mikhailovich made on me at our first meeting. I thought he looked absent-minded, terribly worried, helpless, lonely, irritated, practically ill. He seemed so crushed by some kind of misfortune that he did not see one's face and was incapable of carrying on a coherent conversation.[2]

Working together, *The Gambler* was finished just in time, and they continued to collaborate on the remaining installments of *Crime and Punishment*. Dostoevsky found himself becoming more and more attached to Anna. On November 8, 1866, barely a month after meeting her, he proposed to Anna Snitkina. He had been longing to remarry and had already proposed to four women — Polina, Anna Korvin-Krulovskaya, Maria Sergeevna-Pisareva and Elena Pavlovna

---

[1] Quoted in Grossman, *Op. Cit.*, pp. 349-50
[2] In Grossman, *Op. Cit.*, p. 394.

Ivanova[1] — before Anna Snitkina accepted his proposal. They were married on February 15, 1867.

Despite the fact that Dostoevsky was now married to a very capable woman, who would be able to handle their finances as he had never been able to handle his own, he was still deeply in debt. After pawning nearly everything, Dostoevsky once again found himself leaving St. Petersburg for Europe to escape his creditors, this time with his wife. They ended up spending four years in Europe, living first in Dresden and then in Baden-Baden, where Dostoevsky succumbed to his gambling obsession. This was a particularly bad time for the Dostoevskys, since Dostoevsky was often ill with seizures, Anna was now nauseous from pregnancy and they were desperately poor.

The winter of 1867-68 was spent in Geneva, working on *The Idiot*, the central character of which, Prince Myshkin, was to be Dostoevsky's representation of a perfect man. Chapters of this book began appearing in the *Russian Messenger* in January 1868.

Three other important events occurred in Geneva. First, Dostoevsky attended meetings of the Geneva Congress where Bakunin's "steely words, calling for the destruction of religion and patriotism, sent stabs of pain into his heart."[2] Second, Dostoevsky's first child, Sonya, named after his favorite niece and the heroine of *Crime and Punishment*, was born on March 5, 1868. He discovered the joys of fatherhood late in life, when he was forty-six. The final event, however, was terrible. Sonya died of pneumonia on May 24th, less than three months after her birth. Dostoevsky's grief was overwhelming. He and his wife left Geneva for Vevey, where they spent the summer; and then in early September they left for Italy, where Dostoevsky finished *The Idiot*.

That spring, they went to Prague, but finding no furnished rooms to rent there, the Dostoevskys went on to Dresden, where they lived for nearly two years. Their second daughter, Lyubov, was born there on September 14, 1969. While in Dresden, Dostoevsky began outlining a large work, tentatively titled *The Life of a Great Sinner*, which was supposed to be at least as long as Leo Tolstoy's 1868 novel *War and Peace* and inspired in part by George Sand's novel *Spiridion*. *Spiridion*, which Dostoevsky had probably first read in the 1840s, had

---

[1] Anna Korvin-Krulovskaya had contributed two stories to *Time*, and he met the last two while on a prolonged visit to his sister Vera Ivanova and her family in the summer of 1866.

[2] Grossman, *Op. Cit.*, p. 431.

raised the issue that continued to fascinate Dostoevsky: the debate between Socialism and Christianity. Although he never finished the entire project — which was supposed to consist of five separate stories, spanning three decades of Russian history, tied together by a common hero — it did generate the material for Dostoevsky's last three novels: *The Devils* (also called *The Possessed*), *A Raw Youth* and *The Brothers Karamazov*.

The last year the Dostoevskys spent in Europe was spent under adverse circumstances. They were in Germany during the entire Franco-Prussian War of 1870. Nevertheless, Dostoevsky began working on the political novel *The Devils*, which was based on the "Nechaev affair," involving a Russian radical student who was murdered by his comrades for not obeying orders. The novel was published in the *Russian Messenger* beginning in early 1871. Also during this year, in April 1871, Dostoevsky experienced a private victory when he was finally able to give up gambling after a heavy loss in Wiesbaden.

The Dostoevskys returned to Russia in July 1871. Their first son, Fyodor, was born on July 26th, just a week afterwards. Although still in debt, the family's financial situation gradually improved, since Dostoevsky had given up gambling and his writings were more successful, and thanks to his wife's good management of his earnings. They were able to spend the summers in Staraya Russa, a spa in the province of Novgorod.

Dostoevsky was now welcomed by conservatives, having clearly criticized Russian liberals in novels like *The Devils*. Prince Meshchersky asked Dostoevsky to become the editor of *The Citizen*, a conservative weekly which he had created, starting in 1873. He accepted the job and it became an outlet for the publication of several of his short stories, as well as his series of essays which he called *The Diary of a Writer*. With this series, Dostoevsky created a new form of literary journalism which included reminiscences, discussions of events of the day and even "incidental stories."

Philosophical differences with Meshchersky, problems with censors, and Dostoevsky's desire to return to working on his novels caused him to resign from his editorship position in March 1874. He then worked on *A Raw Youth*, which was published in *Notes of the Fatherland* beginning in early 1875. In the same year, Dostoevsky's second son, and last child, was born, when Alyosha arrived in August. *The Diary of a Writer* was revived at the beginning of 1876 as an independent monthly publication.

The last years of Dostoevsky's life were not as eventful as earlier years. He enjoyed his family and the hard-fought fame he finally achieved, and his creative talents were at their peak. In the summer of 1878, he began writing his great masterpiece, *The Brothers Karamazov*, "a novel of synthesis, summing up almost the whole of the writer's work and striving to embody all his most cherished thoughts."[1] *The Brothers Karamazov* was published in the *Russian Messenger* through the year 1879 and into 1880.

Although his health was failing, Dostoevsky traveled to Moscow to give a speech on June 8, 1880 on the occasion of the unveiling of a monument to Pushkin. In his impassioned address, Dostoevsky emphasized the important role of artistic geniuses, like Pushkin, to the future of mankind, maintained that the intelligentsia could benefit from "humble association with the common people," and looked forward to universal harmony in the future. Gleb Uspensky, in his article "The Pushkin Celebrations," wrote of the reception Dostoevsky received: "The moment Dostoevsky finished, the audience gave him — an ovation is not the word — they went into ecstasies of idolization."[2]

On January 28, 1881 Dostoevsky died after hemorrhaging off and on for two days, brought on by a quarrel with his favorite sister over inheritance rights. He was buried in the Tichvin Cemetery of the Alexander Nevsky Monastery, with a huge crowd in attendance. Vladimir Solovyov, who was close to Dostoevsky at the end of his life, said that "Russia has not merely lost a writer, she has lost her spiritual leader." He said, further, conveying Dostoevsky's message to the different factions in Russia:

> And as we unite in our love for him, let us do our utmost to see to it that this love can also contribute to our reconciliation. Only then shall we be able to give the leader of the Russian people something in return for his works and his great sufferings.[3]

This did not come to pass. Only a month later, Tsar Alexander II met his death at the hand of revolutionaries.

---

[1] Grossman, *Op. Cit.*, p. 575.

[2] Quoted in Grossman, *Op. Cit.*, p. 598.

[3] Quoted in Geir Kjetsaa, *Fyodor Dostoevsky, A Writer's Life*, Viking, New York, 1987, p. 376 and p. 382.

3

The Double and *Notes from Underground*

Here's a man on his way to destruction, a man is losing his identity, and he can hardly control himself.... (*The Double*[1])

[A] man, whoever he is, always and everywhere likes to act as he chooses....it does at any rate preserve what is dear and extremely important to [him], that is [his] personality and [his] individuality. (*Notes from Underground*[2])

In the first two novels I shall discuss, *The Double* (1846) and *Notes from Underground* (1864), Dostoevsky begins to formulate an answer to the question: What is the human predicament? His answer to this question, which is only partially given in *The Double* and presented more completely in *Notes from Underground*, gives us the foundation upon which Dostoevsky's entire philosophy rests.

---

[1] *Notes from Underground and The Double*, translated by Jessie Coulson, Penguin Books, New York, 1972, p. 265.
[2] *Ibid.*, pp. 33-36.

Many years after writing *The Double*, in November of 1877, Dostoevsky wrote that although there were problems with the "form" of this early novel, "its idea was rather lucid, and I have never expressed in my writings anything more serious."[1] The novel is about an ordinary office worker by the name of Yakov Petrovich Golyadkin, a titular counselor whose job was to copy official documents, who gradually went insane after an exact double of himself (physically at least) began to make an appearance in his life.

Before this occurred, Golyadkin was apparently the butt of his fellow workers' jokes. He was too anxious to please others, a coward, a gossip, and inclined to put the blame for his own failures on others. He hated these attributes, but he could not see that he possessed them himself. He seemed satisfied enough with himself at the beginning of the story. On the first page of the novel we are told that, when Golydakin awakened and looked at himself in the mirror, "its owner was evidently quite satisfied with all he saw there."

Then one evening his self-respect was destroyed when he was scorned, humiliated, and physically ejected from a birthday party in honor of Clara Olsufyevna, the daughter of the venerable State Councillor Olsufi Ivanovich and the woman he secretly hoped to marry. He had taken great care with his own appearance, rented a uniform for his lackey of a servant, and hired a fancy carriage for the entire day, only to have it end with his "collaps[ing] into a chair, insensible with horror."

There were signs that all was not completely well with Golyadkin, even that he might create a double, before the party fiasco. Upon encountering his boss the morning of the party, while riding in the carriage which was inappropriate for someone of his social standing, Golyadkin didn't know how to react:

> Mr. Golyadkin, seeing that Andrey Philippovich had recognized him beyond doubt and was staring with all his might, so that he could not remain concealed, blushed to the roots of his hair. 'Ought I to bow? Should I speak to him or not? Ought I to acknowledge our acquaintance?' our hero wondered in indescribable anguish. 'Or shall I pretend it's not me but somebody else strikingly like me, and look as if nothing's the matter?'[2]

---

[1] *The Diary of a Writer*, 1877, *Op. Cit.*, p. 883.
[2] *The Double*, *Op. Cit.*, p. 132.

Immediately after this incident, Golyadkin quite suddenly decided to visit his doctor, Christian Ivanovich Rutenspitz. He was extremely flustered during this visit and the doctor told him that "you require a radical transformation of your whole life and, in a certain sense, a change in your character." Golyadkin seemed, even in the doctor's office, on the verge of a Jekyll-Hyde transformation:

> ...Mr. Golyadkin was undergoing a strange transformation. His grey eyes had a curious shine, his lips twitched, every muscle and every feature of his face seemed to be in fluid motion. He was shaking from head to foot.[1]

At the end of the visit, Golyadkin deliberately misunderstood a question the doctor asked about where he was "formerly living," replying with the following:

> 'I was living, Christian Ivanovich, I was living even formerly. I must have been, mustn't I?' answered Mr. Golyadkin, accompanying his words with a little laugh, and slightly disconcerting Christian Ivanovich with his reply.[2]

Following Golyadkin's other strange behavior during his impromptu visit to the doctor, this seems to be more than just a bit of humor, particularly since Golyadkin was not known to be a humorous fellow. He seemed to be questioning his existence up until that point and ready to forge a new identity. Just a few lines later, as he left the doctor's office, we are told that Golyadkin was "conscious of his freedom."

He continued to behave bizarrely throughout the day. When he ran into some clerks from his office in a restaurant, and they asked him how he came "to be scented and pomaded like this, and all dressed up," his reply was:

> 'Because I choose, gentleman! That is enough!...You all know me, gentlemen, but up until now you have only known one side of me. Nobody is to blame for that, and I admit it is partly my own fault.'[3]

---

[1] *The Double, Op. Cit.*, p. 138.

[2] *Ibid.*, p. 143.

[3] *Ibid.*, p. 147.

On the way to the party, "he was preparing himself for something very worrying, to say the least...." When he arrived at the party, he was refused admittance, forced himself in anyway, and then, realizing the untenableness of his situation:

> Mr. Golyadkin found himself mentally entertaining the desire to sink through the ground or hide himself, together with his carriage, in a mouse-hole. It seemed to him that everything whatever in Olsulfi Ivanovich's house was staring at him through the windows. He knew that if he turned around he would die on the spot.[1]

Golyadkin started to leave, stopping first to stand in a corner of the back hall. He thought about returning to the party but, in a moment of self-enlightenment, said to himself:

> No, what's the use of going in, with a character like mine? What a mean-spirited creature! I ran like a rabbit. Cowardice is my specialty! Base behaviour is always my specialty, no question about it.[2]

However, he then suddenly "stepped forward, as if somebody had touched a spring inside him," went into the ballroom where the guests were assembled and made a total fool of himself, thus causing himself to be ejected from the house.

It seems fairly clear that Golyadkin could no longer live with that self which ended up being so humiliated, and as a result he "invented" a double to whom he gave all his undesirable characteristics, while he tried to hold on to an image of himself as a person with the opposite, "good" qualities:

> Well, then he'll be a scoundrel, and I'll be honest, and people will say, "*That* Golyadkin's a scoundrel, pay no attention to him, and don't get him mixed up with the other; now he's honest, virtuous, modest, gentle, utterly trustworthy at work, and deserving of promotion," — that's how it will be![3]

---

[1] *The Double, Op. Cit.,* p. 151.
[2] *Ibid.,* p. 158.
[3] *Ibid.,* p. 212.

A battle ensued, however, between the two "selves" — with the double, Golyadkin Jr., frustrating everything Golyadkin Sr. tried to do — which eventually culminated in Golyadkin being dragged off to a mental institution.

Bielinsky was critical of *The Double* for not being realistic enough. In particular, he was bothered by the fact that Golyadkin didn't have a good reason for being so troubled and behaving so bizarrely. Unlike the hero of Dostoevsky's first novel, *Poor Folk*, Golyadkin had a good job and enough money:

> He could very well live in the world comfortably, but a pathological suspiciousness and sensitivity to insult are the dark demons of his character, and these demons make a hell of his existence.[1]

Similarly another critic, N. K. Mikhaylovsky, complained:

> Why did the second Golyadkin appear? There are no satisfactory reasons for his appearance in that corner of life which *The Double* represents. Golyadkin Jr. is dragged in by force and against the living truth.[2]

What these comments reveal is the difference between earlier views of the human predicament and the newly emerging existentialist view. The earlier view, most clearly expressed in the philosophy of John Locke (1632 - 1704), was that at birth the mind of a person is a blank slate which is then gradually filled with the experiences the person has during his or her lifetime. Thus, persons are created by their environment. Human beings play, essentially, a passive role in this process.[3]

This view began to change at the end of the eighteenth century when Immanuel Kant (1724 - 1804) shifted the focus from the external world to the *subject* who perceives and acts in it. This was his "Copernican revolution" in philosophy. Kant gave us a new conception of the mind, one in which the mind actively forms what it experiences

---

[1] Quoted in Edward Wasiolek, *Dostoevsky, The Major Fiction*, The M.I.T. Press, Cambridge, Mass., 1964, p. 5.

[2] Wasiolek, *Op. Cit.*, p. 6

[3] We are able to compare, and so generalize from experiences, but not generate new experiences on our own.

through the innate structures of the *forms of intuition*, i.e. everything is perceived in a three-dimensional space and a two-dimensional time; and the *categories of the understanding,* the most important of which is causality, i.e. every event must have a cause. Although Kant made the subject more important than ever before in philosophy, he was interested in the subject in a general way. According to Kant, we all share the same perceptual apparatus. He further maintained that we should all arrive at the same correct way of thinking on ethical matters. Kant's philosophy did not allow for individual differences.

In the nineteenth century, three men writing independently pushed Kant's inward shift still further. First, Søren Kierkegaard (1813 -1855) completed the move to radical subjectivity which was to form the basis of the existentialist philosophy of the twentieth century. Kierkegaard refused to speak of individuals collectively. He believed that we each have the freedom to choose what we will believe and how we will justify our lives.[1] Later in the nineteenth century, Friedrich Nietzsche (1844-1900), added an internal motivating force, the *will to power*, to explain why we act and perceive the world as we do. He also maintained that there are two very different types of persons. There are naturally strong-willed persons (*masters*), whose will to power takes the form of trying to make the most of their own abilities, in the process of which they create their own values. Then there are the more numerous weak-willed persons (*slaves*), whose will to power takes the form of banding together to devise ways of knocking down the masters, whose strength of will they both fear and envy, so that in this negative way they can improve their own position relative to the masters.

Dostoevsky, as we shall see, accepts the radically subjective freedom that Kierkegaard thought we all have and that Nietzsche thought only the masters are capable of having. He also seems to accept an internal motivating force to explain human behavior which is something like Nietzsche's will to power, but, for Dostoevsky, it is the *desire for self-respect* which is crucial. What Dostoevsky further adds to these ideas that is different is that there are desires, characteristics, within each person that are at war with one another.[2] Thus Dostoevsky

---

[1] See my book *On Kierkegaard*, also in the Wadsworth Philosophers Series, for a fuller discussion of Kierkegaard's philosophy.

[2] Nietzsche maintained that, within the master type of person, there may be slave values at war with master values, but the slave values come from *without*, rather than *within* the self.

found, when he looked into the self, not simplicity, but complexity. The subjective viewpoint is a not simple one. This is a major source of problems for human beings, according to Dostoevsky. He also introduces two views which will later become important themes in Jean-Paul Sartre's philosophy: (1) Since we are social creatures, other people's view of us influences how we see ourselves, for better or worse. So, for Dostoevsky, others play a part in determining whether or not we have self-respect. (2) We have a tendency to deny our freedom to escape from the burden of responsibility associated with it. (This anticipates Sartre's notion of *bad faith*.)

To return to *The Double*. There *are* motivating factors behind Golyadkin's feeling the need to create a double: Golyadkin has conflicting impulses within himself which he cannot reconcile with one another and so combine into a single self,[1] and he isn't happy with the view of himself which he sees reflected in others' eyes. He has lost his self-respect. These factors are different from the ones Bielinsky and Mikaylovsky expected would need to be present to drive an ordinary person insane. They thought that only dire poverty or others' brutally mistreating us could cause such a thing. Dostoevsky is giving us a new view of what most troubles human beings, a new view of the human predicament. The locus of evil — that which causes us to suffer — lies in us. It is not a product of the environment, but it can be "encouraged or discouraged by environment."[2] For Dostoevsky, human beings are quite capable of torturing themselves. Golyadkin Jr., the double to whom Golyadkin Sr. gave all the qualities that he hated in himself, ends up persecuting Golyadkin Sr., and so we can say that Golyadkin tortures himself.

At one point in the novel, Petrushka, Golyadkin's servant who has clearly had enough of his master's strange behavior, says: "I shall go to some good people....Good people live honestly, good people live without any faking, and they never come double...."[3] The trouble is that, according to Dostoevsky, none of us is entirely good. We all have good and evil in us, and so we all are *at least* double. Besides being

---

[1] This novel can also be read as a pioneering work which anticipates the work done on multiple personalities sixty years later. See, in particular, Morton Prince, *The Dissociation of a Personality*, Greenwood, New York, 1969 (first published in 1906).

[2] See Robert Louis Jackson, *The Art of Dostoevsky*, Princeton University Press, Princeton, N. J., 1981, p. 9.

[3] *The Double, Op. Cit.*, p. 222. (The sets of periods are in the text.)

concerned that others would think that Golyadkin Jr. was the *real* Golyadkin and Golyadkin Sr. the impostor, what Golyadkin feared most was that there might be an infinite number of Golyadkins.[1]

What can we learn from this early novel which represents Dostoevsky's first pass at depicting the human predicament? In addition to maintaining that we are not simple, that we have conflicting desires within us, Dostoevsky appears to be saying that we determine the world we experience. Golyadkin's world is full of intrigues and enemies, because *his mind* has imposed this on reality. Also, we are able to create a new self, to make changes to ourselves, if we are not happy with what we have been up until now. We are not creatures whose attributes are set in stone. In Golyadkin's case, it is the creation of *Golyadkin Sr.*, not Golyadkin Jr., whom we should focus on. Golyadkin came to realize, at least unconsciously, that he had no respect for the person he had been and so he tried to turn himself into someone more admirable: "I am no intriguer, and I'm proud to say it. Honest, straightforward, orderly, agreeable, mild...."[2] His device for changing himself was to create the double with the undesirable characteristics, allowing him to develop into a better person.

Golyadkin had an amazing amount of freedom, which he, on a few occasions, realized. For the most part, though, he described what happened to him in fatalistic terms: "none of this is my fault. We must blame fate for the whole thing." (He was also optimistic in his fatalism: "it may still all turn out for the best" was his "favorite sentiment.") When the going got rough, Golyadkin denied his freedom.

We also notice that Golyadkin was not successful in overcoming his problems by trying to distance himself from what he had been and by pretending that he had no control over what was happening to him. At the time that *The Double* was written, Dostoevsky was not able to answer the second important question he set for himself: Given that the human predicament is what it is, how then should we live our lives? Later novels will provide an answer to this important question; but in *The Double*, and *Notes From Underground* as well, he gives us only answers which must be rejected. But, of course, rejected answers give us hints about how we *should* live. In *The Double*, Dostoevsky tells us that we should *not* try to deny a part of ourselves, of what we have been; and we should *not* deny our freedom.

---

[1] See Golyadkin's dream about this on pp. 230-1 of the novel.

[2] *The Double, Op. Cit.*, p. 184.

There was an eighteen year gap between *The Double* and *Notes from Underground*. During that interval, Dostoevsky had paid a heavy price for his early attraction to Socialism and he had been to Europe and seen, particularly in the "Crystal Palace" exhibition in London, the disturbing direction — disturbing for him anyway — in which social reformers hoped to take society. We can clearly see the influence of these experiences on *Notes from Underground*.

The novel is divided into two long chapters: "The Underground" and "A Story of the Falling Sleet." Here is how Dostoevsky summarized the contents of the two chapters:

> In the chapter entitled 'The Underground' [the imaginary author] introduces himself and his outlook on life, and tries, as it were, to elucidate the causes that brought about...his appearance in our midst. In the second section we follow this personage's memoirs of some of the happenings in his life.[1]

In the first chapter, we become acquainted with the author of the *Notes*, our "anti-hero," as Dostoevsky refers to him. He is a forty-year-old, former low-level civil servant who lives alone and has no friends. He is ill; but, masochistically, he refuses help: "I am a sick man...I refuse treatment out of spite....I know better than anybody that I am harming nobody but myself." He has thumbed his nose at the establishment: "I was a bad civil servant. I was rude and I enjoyed being rude." He has refused to accept the limits which others seem to accept: "A wall is for them something calming, morally decisive and final," whereas "I have always resented the laws of nature more than anything else."

He has rejected society's values: "The more aware I was of beauty and of 'the highest and the best', the deeper I sank into my slime." He has even enjoyed harming others: "I was hugely delighted when I succeeded in hurting somebody's feelings." But he is not all bad. Again, Dostoevsky insists that human beings are complex:

> [I]n reality I never could make myself [completely] malevolent. I was always conscious of many elements showing the directly opposite tendency. I felt them positively

---

[1] *Notes from Underground, Op. Cit.*, p. 13.

swarming inside me, these elements. I knew they had swarmed there all my life, asking to be let out....[1]

He is very intelligent — "I am cleverer than anybody else around me" — but realizes that "to think too much is a disease,"[2] in part because it leads to inaction: "[I]n order to act, one must be absolutely sure of oneself, no doubts must remain anywhere;" but a person who thinks too much will always have doubts. He is an overly sensitive "man of heightened awareness" in whom resentments[3] for imagined slights have festered for years. It is this which led him to "deliberately bury" himself "in a cellar for forty years out of spite." He recognizes that his real problem lies in his "having no respect for [him]self," and now he has "no other occupation than nursing [his] self-esteem."

Our anti-hero presents his philosophy of life, and it is clear that it is Dostoevsky's own. Dostoevsky attacks deterministic views of human behavior, in particular the view of Psychological Egoism, that all human beings always act in the way which they believe is in their own best interest. Dostoevsky had just read the novel by the socialist N. G. Chernyshevsky, *What is to be Done?* (1863), which had argued that an ideal society could be achieved by rationally demonstrating that it is in each individual's own self interest to cooperate with the rest, to act in a way which is "virtuous and noble." The argument assumed that we always act in a self-interested manner.

Dostoevsky believes that people can, and do, act against their own self-interest. They have deliberately sabotaged their own interests on occasions, just to thwart expectations, because "obstinacy and self-will meant more to them than any kind of advantage." Dostoevsky claims that there is "something that is dearer to almost every man than his own very best interests" and that is "[o]ne's own free and unfettered volition, one's own caprice."

It is clear that Dostoevsky is not only rejecting the specific deterministic theory of Psychological Egoism, but *any* deterministic theory of human behavior. He believes that human beings don't behave consistently. We refuse to be bound to any "laws of nature" which

---

[1] *Notes from Underground, Op. Cit.*, p. 16.

[2] This is a new theme for Dostoevsky, and it will become increasingly important to his overall philosophy.

[3] The crucial role that resentment plays in human psychology is an important idea for Nietzsche as well. This is undoubtedly one of the reasons why Nietzsche found a kindred spirit in Dostoevsky.

social scientists try to impose on us. We have free will and will use it even to do "what is positively harmful and stupid." Why?

> [B]ecause it does at any rate preserve what is dear and extremely important to us, that is our personality and our individuality. Some would assert that it is indeed what is dearest of all to man....[1]

Dostoevsky believes that we are free in the *libertarian* sense, which means that we are able to perform alternative actions, without altering the antecedent conditions, and that we are the sole cause of the action which is chosen. I may choose to jump up and down at this moment, or I may choose not to do so. If I choose to do so, I will; and if I don't, I won't. This libertarian conception of free will is incompatible with *Determinism*, the view that every event — including all human actions — must inevitably occur, given the antecedent conditions. Determinism insists that all human actions are in principle predictable, because there are causal laws governing human behavior. This is precisely what Dostoevsky denies.

He acknowledges that there is another view of free will, one that is compatible with Determinism and which has become very popular in an age in which faith in science inclines many scholars to think deterministically. This second view of free will, called the *compatibilist* conception, maintains that we act freely as long as we do not act under compulsion, as long as we are able to translate our desires into action. Since, most of the time, it is my own desires which determine what my actions will be, I can be said to be acting freely, even if Determinism is true and I could not do otherwise. Thus we can say, assuming the truth of Determinism, that I act freely in jumping up and down at this moment, even though I couldn't do otherwise, because this is what I wished to do. No one forced me to do so against my will. But Dostoevsky rejects this view of free will. To him, it is not free will at all. He says that "if the formula for all our desires and whims is some day discovered," that is if Determinism is someday proven to be true, then human beings as we think of them will cease to exist. Man "will at once turn from a man into a barrel-organ sprig or something of the sort." We would be no different, in principle, from ordinary physical objects whose behavior is entirely predictable. But Dostoevsky insists that we *are* different. Above all else, according to Dostoevsky, our

---

[1] *Notes from Underground, Op. Cit.,* p. 36.

existence as human beings boils down to our demonstrating to ourselves through our actions that, unlike other objects in the universe, we have *free will*. What we do is *not* determined:

> [I]t seems to me that the whole business of humanity consist solely in this — that a man should constantly prove to himself that he is a man and not a sprig in a barrel-organ! To prove it even at the expense of his own skin....[1]

Dostoevsky, therefore, recommends that we "send all [the supposed causal laws governing human behavior] to the devil and...live our own lives at our own sweet will."

What Dostoevsky finds so objectionable about socialist utopian proposals to bring about the ideal society, symbolized for him by the "Crystal Palace," is that they assume that human beings have a definable nature, that, in particular, they necessarily seek their own happiness; all that remains to do is to rationally show them how to reach the desired goal. Then "all problems will vanish in the twinkling of an eye." But Dostoevsky maintains that we are capricious creatures. We will use our free will, which is what enables us to express our individuality, to thwart any attempt by others to use reason to tell us what we are and ought to be. He believes that history shows his view of human nature to be correct: "anything can be said of world history....There is only one thing that you can't say — that it had anything to do with reason."

Another view which Dostoevsky is attacking, besides Socialism, is Hedonistic Utilitarianism, a philosophy that was becoming increasingly popular in England in the nineteenth century. According to this view, advocated by Jeremy Bentham and John Stuart Mill, all human beings desire to increase their own pleasure or happiness, and decrease their own suffering or unhappiness. Since we each desire this, and no one of us should count any more than the others, the ideal is whatever course of action brings about the greatest net pleasure or happiness, for the greatest number.[2] Against this, Dostoevsky says that "[man] is just as attracted to suffering....I am certain that man will never deny himself

---

[1] *Notes from Underground, Op. Cit.*, p. 38.
[2] For a thorough discussion of Bentham's and Mill's views see my book *On Mill*, also in the Wadsworth Philosophers Series.

destruction and chaos. Suffering — after all, that is the sole cause of consciousness."[1]

We can begin to see in *Notes from Underground*, Dostoevsky's mounting criticism of socialists, and even liberals like Bentham and Mill. As Lawrence Stern summarizes Dostoevsky's reasoning, they "seek institutional solutions for the problems of mankind."[2] Individuals are, in the process, deprived of their free will. Dostoevsky does not disagree with the ideal of more equality and cooperation, but he thinks that it must *come from within* individuals. They must freely choose it. Equality of condition cannot be imposed on them; they will simply rebel against being told what to do, just as our anti-hero has done.

Towards the end of the first chapter we are told that the anti-hero realizes that to live one's life in the underground is not the ideal. He would like to leave it, but doesn't think he'll ever find his way out:

> I know...that it isn't the underground that is better, but something different, entirely different, which I am eager for, but which I shall never find. Devil take the underground![3]

In the second chapter of *Notes from Underground*, "A Story of the Falling Sleet," we learn of three episodes in our anti-hero's life, which happened some twenty years before, of which he is not proud and which led to his loss of self-respect. As the Underground Man describes these incidents in the context of his life, we become aware of the fact that, despite his intellectual conviction that we have free will, he has a tendency to view his own life deterministically. Again, Dostoevsky is telling us that we are often guilty of denying our freedom, the most precious gift we possses. Consider, for instance, this typical passage demonstrating the way in which the anti-hero saw his life:

> I very often looked at myself with frantic dislike, sometimes amounting to disgust, and therefore attributed the same attitude to everybody else. For example, I hated my face, I thought it was a scoundrelly face, and I even suspected there was something servile about it, and so every time I went to the

---

[1] *Notes from Underground, Op. Cit.*, p. 41.

[2] Lawrence Stern, "Freedom and Love in *Notes from Underground*," *Philosophy Research Archives*, Vol. 4, 1978, p. G-3.

[3] *Notes from Underground, Op. Cit.*, p. 43.

office, I made agonizing attempts to seem as independent as possible, so that I should not be suspected of subservience....[1]

He didn't like himself, and felt subservient, which he traced back to having lost his parents early in life and then having been left in the care of unfeeling distant relatives who sent him off to a school where he had terrible experiences. As a result, he inevitably saw other people as trying to put him down, which would lead him to behave inappropriately in an attempt to regain the upper hand.

The first incident he describes began one night in a tavern when he found himself accidentally blocking the path of an officer. The much taller officer moved him aside to get by. This made the Underground Man feel like he "had been treated like an insect." Resentment seethed inside him for years — he was obsessed with it — before he was finally able to get his "revenge" in an unsatisfactory manner.

The second incident began when, feeling lonely, he visited a former classmate whom he found with two other former classmates planning a going away party for a fourth classmate. He invited himself to the party, even though he knew that he wasn't wanted and he didn't particularly want to go. He arrived an hour too early — they had no way to inform him of a change in the time — causing him to feel humiliated and behave abominably towards the other three. They simply ignored him. Unable to bear being "snubbed" in this way, and feeling "terribly ashamed," he borrowed money to follow the others to a brothel, determined to "redeem [his] position" somehow: "I will redeem it, or perish on the spot this very night."

At the brothel, he met the prostitute Liza. The third, and most important, incident he relates involved his treatment of her. Unable to get revenge on his classmates for his loss of self-esteem, he takes it out instead on this "kind and simple-hearted" girl, who is down on her luck. Even after having had his way with her, when he awakened later he found that "[a]nger and misery seethed up" inside him again, "seeking an outlet." He lectured her at length on the dangers of her sordid life. The bleak picture he presented devastated Liza: "never had I witnessed such despair!" At that point, feeling remorse, he said to her, "Here is my address, Liza; come to me." She said that she would. Before he left, she showed him her "treasure," a declaration of love written by a young medical student whom she'd met, who didn't know her occupation. She wanted our anti-hero to know:

---

[1] *Notes from Underground, Op. Cit.*, p. 47.

that she was loved, honourably and sincerely, and that people spoke to her with respect. The letter was almost certainly destined to remain put away, without consequences. But that didn't matter; I'm sure she would treasure it all her life....[1]

Afterwards, the Underground Man was troubled by the thought that Liza would visit him and discover that he lived in poverty. When she showed up, he was in the middle of a humilating quarrel with his servant who had, as usual, gotten the upper hand with his master. Again he felt compelled to "make her pay dearly" for having seen him at his worst. He lashed out at her. But Liza understood that he was unhappy and she held out her arms to him. They cried together; then the Underground Man felt ashamed. He realized that their "roles had definitely been reversed," that "she was the heroine" and he was "just such another crushed and degraded creature as she had been" before. In a rage, he possessed her again sexually, finally showing her that he was "a vile creature and, most important, not in a condition to love her." He spitefully forced money into her hand, which she left behind. He was deliberately cruel to her, but "it came from [his] wicked head, not from [his] heart." He never saw her again, preferring "to be left in peace, alone in his underground." He concluded that his was "a long story about how [he] missed life through decaying morally in a corner...losing the habit of living, and carefully cultivating [his] anger underground."[2]

In this story Dostoevsky states very clearly that we are free to live the lives we choose. No one can take that away from us. But we are afraid of this freedom: "Just try giving us as much independence as possible...I assure you that we should all immediately beg to go back under discipline."[3] Further complicating our situation is the fact that we have conflicting impulses within us, some good and some bad; and we will do almost anything to salvage some measure of self-respect, if we feel that we've lost it. So it often happens that we lose our way. Our anti-hero rejected love, which might have saved him, believing that he was incapable of loving anyone. Like Golyadkin, he didn't use the freedom he had properly; and, also like Golyadkin, he denied his freedom. But this time we are given a hint as to how we should live. Liza, the heroine of the story, knew that it is important to love.

---

[1] *Notes from Underground, Op. Cit.*, p. 102.

[2] *Ibid.*, p. 122.

[3] *Ibid.*

4

Crime and Punishment

In the *Notes* the Underground Man had reasoned out the terrifying consequences of being unfree; in *Crime and Punishment* Raskolnikov acts out the terrifying consequences of being free. (Edward Wasiolek[1])

"This is a murky, fantastic case, a contemporary one, an incident that belongs to our own age, an age in which the heart of man has grown dark and muddied...in which material comfort is preached as life's only aim. It is a case that involves dreams derived from books...a heart that has been overstimulated by theories....He killed, killed two people, because of a theory." (Inspector Porfiry Petrovich in *Crime and Punishment*[2])

---

[1] Edward Wasiolek, *Dostoevsky, The Major Fiction*, The M.I.T. Press, Cambridge, Mass., 1964, p. 67.
[2] *Crime and Punishment*, translated by David McDuff, Penguin Books, New York, 1991, p. 52.

Crime and Punishment picks up where *Notes from Underground* left off. The central character, Rodion Romanovich Raskolnikov[1], a poverty-stricken twenty-three-year-old ex-student, is a "spiritual relative of the Underground Man."[2] But in the progression from *Notes from Underground* to *Crime and Punishment*, the rebellion of the solitary, arrogant individual against the "walls" erected by nature and society moves from *thought* into *action*.[3] In *Notes from Underground*, Dostoevsky established that human beings are essentially free; in *Crime and Punishment*, he shows us possible terrible consequences of that freedom. Human beings are free to commit horrendous crimes. Raskolnikov murders two people early in *Crime and Punishment*. We want to know why and how it could have been prevented.

The story of *Crime and Punishment* is so familiar that I will just briefly summarize the plot and introduce the central characters. We follow the progress of Raskolnikov's mental state as he kills a rich, elderly pawnbroker, who preyed on others' poverty, and is then forced to kill her simple, meek sister when she catches him in the act. After committing his crime, Raskolnikov's "punishment" begins as he not only must deal with his own mental deterioration following the murders, but also with Inspector Porfiry who is certain that he will "get his man," that at some point the murderer will want to confess in order to end his mental torment:

> Have you ever watched a moth near a candle-flame? Well, that's the way he'll be with me, hovering, circling around me like a moth at a lighted candle; he'll lose his taste for freedom, he'll start to think, get tangled in his thoughts....on he'll go, performing a circular orbit around me, narrowing the radius further and further, until — plop! He'll fly straight into my mouth and I'll swallow him whole![4]

Before eventually confessing, Raskolnikov has encounters with several admirable characters who bring out the better side of his nature:

---

[1] "Raskolnikov" derives from the Russian word "Raskol'nik" which means "a dissident."

[2] David McDuff, Introduction to *Crime and Punishment*, *Op. Cit.*, pp. 15-16.

[3] Or more *extreme* action, if you consider the underground man to have acted when, for example, he mistreated Liza.

[4] *Crime and Punishment*, p. 401.

his mother, sister, friend Razumikhin, and the destitute Marmeladov family, particularly Sonya Marmeladov. He also encounters reprehensible characters who act as negative role models: his sister's egoistic fiancé, Luzhin, and her former immoral employer, Svidrigailov. It is Sonya who convinces him that he must confess, and she follows him to Siberia to share his punishment with him. She, too, is a social outcast, having been forced by poverty into prostitution to help her family.

Early in the novel we learn that, just like the Underground Man, Raskolnikov has become "absorbed in himself" and chosen to set himself apart from society: "he felt as though, with a pair of scissors, he had cut himself off from everyone and everything."[1] He is living in a dismal little room which he is reluctant to leave. And it is clear that his is a *self*-incarceration. Just like the Underground Man, he has imprisoned himself out of spite:

> I turned spiteful....And then like a spider, I crept away and hid in my corner....you've been in my rat-hole, you've seen it....Yet even though I hated it, I didn't want to leave it.[2]

Like the Underground Man, Raskolnikov has an urge "to stick out [his] tongue" at the establishment.[3] Furthermore, he, too, dislikes his fellow human beings: "He found all the people he met repulsive — their faces, their manner of walking, their movements were repulsive to him."[4] Consider his impression of the pawnbroker he kills:

> She was a tiny, dried-up little old woman of about sixty, with sharp, hostile eyes, a small, sharp nose....Wound round her long, thin neck, which resembled the leg of a chicken, was an old flannel rag of some description, and from her shoulders...hung an utterly yellowed and motheaten fur jacket.[5]

---

[1] *Crime and Punishment*, p. 157.

[2] *Ibid.*, p. 485.

[3] See *Notes from Underground*, p. 43, and *Crime and Punishment*, p. 209.

[4] *Crime and Punishment*, p. 152.

[5] *Ibid.*, p. 37.

It is easier to kill a person whom one finds repulsive and whom one thinks of merely as "a louse — a loathsome, useless, harmful louse."[1]

As Philip Rahv points out, Raskolnikov spends most of his time "brooding in his cupboard of a room." Just like the Underground Man, "he is filled with the wrath of outraged pride and a furious impatience to break out from his trapped existence even at the risk of self destruction."[2]

If there is any doubt in the reader's mind that Raskolnikov is the Underground Man's heir, the one who *acts* on some of the thoughts of the Dostoevsky's earlier anti-hero, Dostoevsky makes it very clear when Raskolnikov has an encounter with a man who had been the first one to call him a murderer and who later tries to confess to the crime himself :

> ...suddenly a figure appeared — that of yesterday's man *from under the ground*....
>
> The man said nothing; then suddenly he bowed deeply to him, almost down to the floor....
>
> 'What are you up to?' Raskolnikov shouted.
>
> 'I'm guilty,' the man articulated quietly.
>
> 'What of?'
>
> 'Evil thoughts.'
>
> They both looked at each other.[3]

So Raskolnikov is a character out of the same mold as the Underground Man, and above all else, the Underground Man believed that human beings are free. But what are we free for? To just perpetually revolt against society and God in order to assert our independence? This certainly won't make us happy. We need some goal, a positive reason for living. The Underground Man lacked such a

---

[1] *Crime and Punishment*, p. 485.

[2] Philip Rahv, "Dostoevsky in *Crime and Punishment*," in *Dostoevsky, A Collection of Critical Essays*, edited by René Wellek, Prentice-Hall, Englewood Cliffs, New Jersey, 1962, p. 24.

[3] *Crime and Punishment*, p. 418. The italics are Dostoevsky's. The bowing down is also significant. It is a recurring theme in Dostoevsky's novels. One bows down to great suffering and to one to whom one feels an affinity. Earlier in *Crime and Punishment*, Raskolnikov bows down to Sonya, saying afterwards, "It wasn't you I was bowing to, but the whole of human suffering." (p. 380)

purpose and this is why, for the most part, he remained a complainer rather than a doer. Raskolnikov realizes that he must *act*: "he must do something...Whatever happened, he must take some action...."[1] The action he decides to take is to commit a terrible crime. Why?

There are a number of factors which seem to motivate Rasknolnikov's crime. He is desperately poor, and without money he will be unable to finish his studies and have any sort of future. He also wants to save his sister from "selling her soul" by marrying a wealthy man she doesn't love in a misguided attempt to help her mother and brother. Furthermore, he is influenced by the new utilitarian thinking of his day, which appears to justify the crime. Finally, Raskolnikov has a theory of his own, one which superficially resembles Nietzsche's, which he thinks validates his breaking society's laws.

Before considering each of these possible reasons why Raskolnikov might have committed his crime, to determine which one truly motivated it, let us ask whether we should exempt him from responsibility for his actions because he is, at least in part, influenced by others' theories and because of the circumstances of his, and his family's poverty. On the contrary, Dostoevsky makes it clear that we are all ultimately responsible for what we do. To view us as merely pawns in the game of life, without free will — "everything proceeds from the environment, and a man is nothing on his own" — takes away all that separates us from animals and inanimate objects. It deprives us of our humanity. Dostoevsky rejects the view that the criminal is not responsible for his crime because it takes away the criminal's freedom, his self-determination, and denies him the punishment that enables him to make amends for his crime and transform himself into a better person. Dostoevsky clearly accepts the retributive theory of punishment which, as Martin Perlmutter states, maintains that:

> [T]he practice of punishment is justified, because the individual who did the wrong "chose" the punishment; in punishing the wrongdoer, we are honoring the individual's choice.
>
> It is demeaning to have our choices treated as if they were something over which we have no control. It is in our interest to be treated as a person, as an autonomous moral agent; we

---

[1] *Crime and Punishment*, p. 79.

ordinarily do want our choices to be respected as emanating from us....[1]

It is clear that Raskolnikov is free — he admits that "everything lies in a man's hands" — although he often denies it: "he suddenly felt that he no longer possessed any freedom of thought or of will, and that everything had suddenly been decided once and for all."[2] He freely committed a terrible crime and now he must pay the price for his actions. It is not a bad thing, in Dostoevsky's eyes, that Raskolnikov has to suffer, for according to Dostoevsky, "suffering...is a great thing ...suffering has a purpose."[3]

Now let us return to the issue of Raskolnikov's motive for committing the murders. Raskolnikov himself realizes that he didn't commit the crime so that he will be able to continue at the university and secure his future. He says to Sonya:

> Look, I told you just now that I was unable to support myself while I was at the university. But you know, I might very well have been able to....But I turned spiteful and refused.[4]

He says, too, that "if the only reason I killed her was because I was hungry...I'd be...*happy* now!"[5] He knows that he wasn't *forced* to murder out of poverty. He also knows that he didn't do it to aid his sister and mother: "I didn't kill in order to help my mother — that's rubbish!"[6] He freely chose to kill for another reason.

Before committing the crime, Raskolnikov overheard a conversation between a student and a young officer, in which the student said:

> [L]ook: on the one hand you have a nasty, stupid, worthless, meaningless, sick old woman who's no use to anyone and is, indeed, actually harmful to people, who doesn't even know

---

[1] Martin Perlmutter, "Desert and Capital Punishment," in *Morality and Moral Controversies*, fourth edition, edited by John Arthur, Prentice-Hall, Upper Saddle River, N. J., 1996, pp. 390 and 396.

[2] *Crime and Punishment*, p. 98.

[3] *Ibid.*, p. 533.

[4] *Ibid.*, p. 485.

[5] *Ibid.*, p. 482.

[6] *Ibid.*, p. 487.

herself why she's alive, and who's going to kick the bucket of her own accord tomorrow....on the other hand you have young fresh energies that are going to waste for want of backing....A hundred, a thousand good deeds and undertakings that could be arranged and expedited with that old woman's money, which is doomed to go to a monastery! Hundreds, possibly even thousands of lives that could be set on the right road; dozens of families saved from poverty....If one were to kill her and take her money, in order with its help to devote oneself to the service of mankind and the common cause: what do you think — wouldn't one petty little crime like that be atoned for by all those thousands of good deeds? Instead of one life — thousands of lives rescued from corruption and decay...there's arithmetic for you![1]

This is clearly a reference to Bentham and Mill's theory of Utilitarianism which maintains that the right action in a given situation is the action which is likely to lead to the greatest net good consequences, taking everyone into account. Some philosophers have been concerned that this theory could be used to justify harming one person to help many others.[2] But is this what motivated Raskolnikov's killing the pawnbroker? No. He tells Sonya: "I didn't kill in order to get money and power and thus be able to become a benefactor of mankind. That's rubbish too!"[3]

Raskolnikov's true motivation can be found in a theory he presented in an article he wrote, in which he divides human beings into "ordinary" people and "extraordinary" people, the latter consisting of the few "who possess a gift or a talent for saying something new." He claimed that, whereas ordinary people must obey the law,

> an "extraordinary" person has a right...not an official right, of course, but a private one, to allow his conscience to step across certain...obstacles, and then only if the execution of his

---

[1] *Crime and Punishment*, pp. 101-2.

[2] This is what led W. D. Ross, in the twentieth century, for example, to separate the duty of non-maleficence (the obligation to cause the least harm) from the duty of beneficence (the obligation to promote as much good as possible) in formulating his ethical theory of prima facie duties, and claim that the first duty is stronger than the second.

[3] *Crime and Punishment*, p. 487.

idea (which may occasionally be the salvation of mankind) requires it.

Raskolnikov added that the extraordinary people are "the lords of the future" and "move the world and lead it towards a goal." In committing his crime, what Raskolnikov wanted to know was whether he was one of the "extraordinary" people, whether he "could take the step across, or whether [he] couldn't...whether [he] had a *right*..."[1]

The theory which motivated Raskolnikov's crime may appear to be very similar to Friedrich Nietzsche's view that people can be divided into "masters" and "slaves", the first group, the truly creative individuals, having the ability and right to choose their own values. There is, however, an important difference between the two views which should be noted. Nietzsche's "master", a potential "overman", desires power only over himself, choosing and acting on his own values so that he can develop his talents to the fullest. Rasknolnikov's "extraordinary" person, on the other hand, wants power over others. Nietzsche's "overman" is an artist, in the broadest sense of the word; Raskolnikov's model of an "extraordinary" person is Napoleon.

In any case, although Raskolnikov was capable of planning and committing his crime,[2] he could not live with the deed afterwards. As Nietzsche said of the "pale man" who killed God, in *Thus Spoke Zarathustra*:

> But thought is one thing, the deed is another, and the image of the deed still another: the wheel of causality does not roll between them.
>
> An image made this pale man pale. He was equal to the deed when he did it; but he could not bear its image after it was done....madness *after* the deed I call this.[3]

---

[1] *Crime and Punishment*, p. 488.

[2] Even in doing the deed, however, he seemed to just go through the motions of the chain of events he had started: "But now this...day, which had dawned...and had decided everything, acted on him in an almost mechanical fashion: as though someone had taken him by the hand and pulled him along behind him....As though a corner of his clothing had got caught in the flywheel of a machine, and he was beginning to be drawn into it." (*Ibid.*, p. 107)

[3] *Thus Spoke Zarathustra*, translated by Walter Kaufmann, Viking, New York, 1972, p. 38.

Nearly a century after Dostoevsky wrote *Crime and Punishment*, Jean-Paul Sartre wrote a play in which this idea of Nietzsche's figured prominently. In Sartre's "The Flies," we have an example of a character, Electra, who can plan to kill her mother and her mother's lover, to avenge the death of her father, but she has trouble doing the deed and certainly cannot live with it afterwards, succumbing to the flies (Furies) in the end who represent remorse. Her brother, Orestes, on the other hand, is able to go through all three stages — think of the deed, do it, and live with it afterwards — without having regrets. He is the hero of that play and one of Sartre's few examples of a character who lives authentically.

Raskolnikov, however, has second thoughts after his deed and this troubles him. He realizes that he is not the exceptional person he thought he was. As Svidrigailov tells Raskolnikov's sister:

> It appears that he...thought he was a man of genius — or at least was convinced of it for a time. He suffered greatly, and is still suffering, from the notion that while he was able to construct a theory, he wasn't able to do the stepping across without reflection, and so consequently is not a man of genius.[1]

If he really believed that his action was right, Raskolnikov would be able to live with his deed afterwards. As Porfiry says of him:

> I think you're one of the kind who even if his intestines were being cut out would stand looking at his torturers with a smile — as long as he's found a God, or a faith.[2]

Raskolnikov hasn't truly found "a God or a faith" which he believes in enough to justify *anything* he does, much less commit murder. Unlike others who have broken society's laws while acting on beliefs they held dear, Raskolnikov lacks the strength of conviction which they had. They, according to him, "had the courage of their convictions, and so *they were right*, while I didn't, and consequently had no right to take the step I did."[3]

---

[1] *Crime and Punishment*, p. 566.

[2] *Ibid.*, p. 532.

[3] *Ibid.*, p. 623.

But is that the only reason why he should not have murdered two people, because he lacked the conviction to completely pull it off? Not according to Dostoevsky, who, unlike Nietzsche and Sartre, accepts the existence of *absolute* values. Dostoevsky rejects the view of *Ethical Relativism* — the view that individuals and/or societies are entitled to have their own codes of values — which underlies the theory Raskolnikov presents in his article and Nietzsche's and Sartre's philosophies. It seems clear, in *Crime and Punishment*, that Dostoevsky sees an act of murder, even of a "louse" like the pawnbroker, much less the innocent Lizaveta, as wrong absolutely. Raskolnikov has, therefore, "reached the moment of justice."[1]

Sonya, the heroine of the story, the one who is able to save Raskolnikov, says: "Who am I to set myself up as a judge of who should live and who should not?"[2] She cuts through the "end justifies the means" utilitarian philosophy and the ethical relativism at the heart of Raskolnikov's theory. When he says "Look Sonya, all I killed was a louse — a loathsome, useless, harmful louse!", her response is simple: "But that louse was a human being!" This prompts Raskolnikov to admit:

> "Oh, I too know that she wasn't really a louse," he replied, looking at her strangely. "Actually, I'm talking nonsense, Sonya," he added, "I've been doing that for a long time now...."[3]

But how can we defend an absolute code of values against the conflicting views of different individuals? Dostoevsky gives us his first glimpse at his answer to this question in *Crime and Punishment*. It will form the basis of his response to the second basic philosophical question he tries to answer: How should we live our lives? We need to look, once again, at Sonya, at her beliefs. She recognizes that we need one another: "how can you live without anyone, without anyone at all?"[4] Sonya is also deeply religious — "What would I be without God?"[5] — and it is her belief in the existence of God which tells her that murder is wrong. From her perspective, Raskolnikov's problem is

---

[1] *Crime and Punishment*, p. 532.

[2] *Ibid.*, p. 476.

[3] *Ibid.*, p. 485.

[4] *Ibid.*, p. 489.

[5] *Ibid.*, p. 383.

that he has "strayed away from God."[1] His mother also realized this. In a letter which Raskolnikov received from her early in the novel, she wrote:

> Do you say your prayers, Rodya, the way you used to, and do you believe in the mercy of the Creator and Our Redeemer? I fear in my heart that you may have been affected by this latest fashion of unbelief. If that's the case, then I pray for you.[2]

Dostoevsky is clearly critical of the atheist reformers who hope to make the world a better place by trampling over some people. Those who abandon God, and the absolute values of religion, according to Dostoevsky, are dangerous.

If we assume that there is a God who gives us an absolute code of values to follow, then Raskolnikov's relativism and his "end justifies the means" thinking become questionable. We can see why his crime must eat away at his heart until he truly repents. He can be seen to suffer from the "sickness unto death" which Kierkegaard said is the fate of the despairing individual who denies his eternal self and the author of this self, God:

> [T]o be sick *unto* death is, not to be able to die — yet not as though there were hope of life....If one might die of despair as one dies of a sickness, then the eternal in him, the self must be capable of dying in the same sense that the body dies of sickness. But this is an impossibility...The despairing man cannot die; no more than "the dagger can slay thoughts" can despair consume the eternal thing, the self, which is the ground of despair...Yet despair is precisely *self*-consuming, but it is an impotent self-consumption which is not able to do what it wills....[3]

But introducing God into the picture, to support absolute values, raises two problems which were to haunt Dostoevsky until his last work, where he was finally able to respond to them: (1) How can we be

---

[1] *Crime and Punishment*, p. 487.

[2] *Ibid.*, p. 73.

[3] Søren Kierkegaard, *The Sickness Unto Death*, in *A Kierkegaard Anthology*, edited by Robert Bretall, Princeton University Press, Princeton, N. J., 1946, pp. 341-2.

free if there is a God? and (2) How can there be a God, when so many innocent beings suffer in this life?

Leaving these problems aside for the moment, it is clear, from Dostoevsky's perspective, that it is not only Raskolnikov's atheism that led to his crime. Raskolnikov's egoism, isolationism, and pride have also contributed.[1] Dostoevsky believes that we need to reach out to one another with compassion and love. We must recognize our bond with our fellow human beings, and to do so we must overcome our pride which is a hindrance to our doing so. In this novel, Dostoevsky introduces the further idea that children can guide us in proper behavior for "children are the image of Christ."[2]

At times Raskolnikov does show kindness to others. Like all of us, he is complex, wrestling with good and evil tendencies within himself.[3] His friend Razumikhin says of him, "it's really just as though there were two opposing characters alternating within him."[4] When he has the dream which is so similar to the incident involving the beating of a horse that Dostoevsky himself witnessed as a young man, Raskolnikov feels compassion for the mare, even as he was about to do something similar to the old pawnbroker. He helps the Marmeladovs and he obviously cares about his mother and sister. At his trial, a number of compassionate actions, which he had performed before we first encounter him, were mentioned which reduced his sentence. But he tends to become upset with himself when his good impulses emerge. He thinks they betray a weakness, rather than a strength. Thus, after he helped a drunken young girl, who had already been molested, from being taken advantage of by a lecher, he thinks "Why did I poke my nose in, trying to help?...Oh, they can swallow each other alive for all I care!"[5]

At the end of the novel, Raskolnikov is saved by Sonya's love — "there was love in that gaze; his hatred vanished like a wraith"[6] — accepting the chance to be reborn which she had earlier offered him when she read the story of Lazarus to him. Although he struggled

---

[1] Of course, according to Dostoevsky, they are related to his atheism.

[2] *Crime and Punishment*, p. 389.

[3] The doctor Zosimov says that "the harmonious individual...hardly exists at all." (*Crime and Punishment*, p. 277)

[4] *Crime and Punishment*, p. 265.

[5] *Ibid.*, p. 84.

[6] *Ibid.*, p. 476.

against it, largely because "his pride had been violently wounded,"[1] he finally realizes that it offers him, and us all, the only hope for a future life of happiness:

> [T]here now gleamed the dawn of a renewed future, a complete recovery to a new life. What had revived them was love, the heart of the one containing an infinite source of life for the heart of the other.[2]

In the end, Raskolnokov emerges as a person who is both worse and better than the Underground Man. He killed two people, which is far worse than the insults the Underground Man was capable of, but he also finally recognizes the value of love and is even open to the possibility of believing in God.[3] He sees that the way to finding meaning in life is not through theories, the intellect — "I went into it like a fellow with some brains, and that was my undoing"[4] — but through feeling: "now he could only feel. In place of dialectics life had arrived."[5] The man who earlier in the novel felt that "it was myself I killed, not the old woman"[6] has the chance for a "gradual rebirth":

> [A]t this point a new story begins, the story of a man's gradual renewal, his gradual rebirth, his gradual transition from one world to another, of his growing acquaintance with a new, hitherto completely unknown reality.[7]

In his remaining works, Dostoevsky will give us glimpses of this "new, hitherto completely unknown reality," which represents the ideal type of life towards which he believes we must aim. He will show us how to properly use our freedom, in addition to continuing to show us how not to use it.

---

[1] *Crime and Punishment*, p. 622.

[2] *Ibid.*, p. 629.

[3] "What if her convictions can now be mine, too?" (*Ibid.*, p. 630)

[4] *Ibid.*, p. 487.

[5] *Ibid.*, p. 630.

[6] *Ibid.*, p. 488.

[7] *Ibid.*, p. 630.

5

The Idiot and *The Devils*

"My dear Prince...it is not easy to achieve heaven on earth, and you do seem to count on it a little: heaven is a difficult matter, Prince, much more difficult than it seems to your excellent heart." (Prince Sh. to Prince Myshkin in *The Idiot*[1])

"You've lost the distinction between good and evil because you no longer know your own people...." (Shatov to Stavrogin in *The Devils*[2])

When he first started writing *The Idiot*, Dostoevsky wrote to the poet Apollon Maykov about its central idea:

For a long time I have been tormented by an idea....The idea is the representation of a perfect man. Nothing in my opinion

---

[1] *The Idiot*, translated by David Magarshack, Penguin Books, New York, 1955, p. 326.
[2] *The Devils*, translated by David Magarshack, Penguin Books, New York, 1971, p. 262.

can be more difficult....I caught fleeting glimpses of this idea
before, but that is not enough.[1]

Dostoevsky did give us "fleeting glimpses" of ideal human behavior, of
the right way to use one's freedom, through the actions of Liza in *Notes
from Underground* and Sonya in *Crime and Punishment*. Neither
character, however, was very well developed. Now, in *The Idiot*,
Dostoevsky tries to make the central character of his novel embody his
vision of how we ought to behave.

The Idiot is the story of a twenty-six year old child-like[2] man,
Prince Leo Nikolayevich Myshkin, who arrives in St. Petersburg from
another country after recovering from a serious illness. Like the
enlightened escaped prisoner in Plato's "Allegory of the Cave"[3] and
Nietzsche's Zarathustra, the Prince believes that he has attained a level
of wisdom others lack and he would like to share his wisdom with
others, hoping to help them to make the most of their lives. But others
react to him just as the unenlightened prisoners reacted to the
enlightened prisoner in Plato's allegory and the people in the
marketplace reacted to Nietzsche's Zarathustra. He is an object of
ridicule — an "idiot" — because he seems to be so out of touch with
what they think is reality, with what they think is important in life.
Zarathustra quickly realized that the general public "do not understand
me; I am not a mouth for these ears."[4] As a result, he decided to
concentrate his efforts only on those few who might able to understand
him. But Prince Myshkin persists in his mission of trying to help all
others, as did Plato's enlightened prisoner; and the Prince, just like the
enlightened prisoner, ends up being destroyed by those whom he tries
to aid.

The people whom the Prince tries to help include: General and
Mrs. Yepanchin (possibly a distant relative) and their three daughters,
Alexandra, Adelaida and Aglaya; the Ivolgins, a proud, poor family,
headed by an impossibly drunken liar; the corrupt but, in his own way,
loyal civil servant Lebedev; Ippolit Terentyev, a young nihilist who is
dying of consumption; the beautiful outcast Nastasya Filippovna and

---

[1] Quoted by Magarshack in his introduction to *The Idiot*, pp. ix-x.

[2] Dostoevsky continues to develop the idea that young children can
show us the way we ought to behave.

[3] See Part III, Book XXV of Plato's *Republic*. Socrates was obviously
Plato's model for the enlightened prisoner.

[4] *Thus Spoke Zarathustra, Op. Cit.*, p. 16.

her on-again, off-again fiancé Parfyon Rogozhin. The Prince decides that Nastasya is the most desperate and needy of them all. He offers to marry her, choosing her over the woman he really loves and who loves him, Aglaya Yepanchin. This results in his being shunned by nearly everyone else and leads to Nastasya's death at the hands of the jealous Rogozhin, which causes his own complete mental breakdown. How is it possible that a man with the most admirable intentions, who is supposed to be Dostoevsky's ideal person, could cause so much harm?

It seems clear that Dostoevsky believes that the present world is not ready to accept his ideal man. By placing his hero in the *real* world, in which he can barely function — "he was a fool, 'who doesn't know the way of the world and has no place in it'"[1] — Dostoevsky is showing us how wide a gap there is between the rest of us, or at least the people of his day, and his ideal person. The Prince's insanity, at the end, was his way of leaving the world in which he did not belong.

Early in the novel, Adelaida Yepanchin guesses the role the Prince will play in the lives of those with whom he comes in contact. She says to him, "You're a philosopher and you've come to instruct us."[2] Mostly by example, but occasionally through mini-lectures, the Prince demonstrates the way Dostoevsky believes we ought to view life and treat others. First, drawing from his own experience of nearly being executed, he maintains that we ought to view every day we live as precious and that we can, and should, be happy:

> Oh, what do my grief and my troubles matter, if I have the power to be happy? You know I can't understand how one can pass by a tree and not be happy at the sight of it! To talk to a man and not be happy in loving him?...think how many beautiful things there are at every step, things even the most wretched man cannot but find beautiful! Look at a child, look at God's sunset, look at the grass, how it grows, look at the eyes that gaze at you and love you....[3]

Concerning our relationships with others, he says that we should not be ashamed to reveal our feelings: "Why are you ashamed of your feelings?....These are your best feelings, so why are you ashamed of

---

[1] *The Idiot*, p. 486.
[2] *Ibid.*, p. 56.
[3] *Ibid.*, p. 531.

them? You only torment yourself, you know."[1] The Prince also recognizes that it is important "to be frank and courteous with everybody."

We should, furthermore, look for what unites us with others, rather than what divides us:

> [V]ery often it only seems that people haven't anything in common, while, in fact, they have — I mean it's just because people are lazy that they are apt to divide themselves into different groups just by looking at one another and can't find any common interests....[2]

The response of the listener to this particular speech given by the Prince illustrates the reaction he generally received. General Yepanchin interrupts the Prince to ask him about a much more important matter as far as the world is concerned: "have you any means at all?"

Since we have much in common — we are all equally human beings — Dostoevsky believes that we should treat one another as equals. Early in the novel, the Prince talks to General Yepanchin's valet as if he were an equal, which is disturbing to the servant since it violates the usual proprieties. The valet concludes that the Prince either has some sort of self-interested motive in being overly friendly or else he has "no sense of personal dignity, for an intelligent prince with a sense of dignity would not be sitting in an ante-room discussing his private affairs with a servant."[3] The latter view was correct, but lacking a sense of personal dignity is not a bad thing for Dostoevsky. He believes that people's sense of personal dignity, of self-respect, often gets in the way of their having ideal relationships with others. Thus, he recommends that, instead of worrying about our dignity, we should be humble: "[The Prince] was quite sincerely ready to believe that, among all those round him, he was morally the lowest of the low."[4]

The fact that the Prince was so humble bothered Aglaya Yepanchin: "Why are you humbling yourself and making yourself out to be inferior to these people?....Why have you no pride?[5] In the current world, it is the case that if you don't feel that you are better than others,

---

[1] *The Idiot*, p. 309.

[2] *Ibid.*, p. 24.

[3] *Ibid.*, p. 17.

[4] *Ibid.*, pp. 247-8.

[5] *Ibid.*, p. 328.

others will think less of you. Dostoevsky recognizes, however, that it is people's pride which causes them to be hurt by others' behavior and to lash out at them in return, setting up a "vicious circle of hurting and being hurt,"[1] which the Prince's humility can break.

Above all, Dostoevsky believes that we should feel compassion for others' suffering. The Prince was attracted to Nastasya from the moment he saw her picture because "there is so much suffering in that face" which "arouse[d] in him a feeling of compassion as he looked at it."[2] Nastasya has led a questionable life, but Dostoevsky believes it is important not to pass judgment on others. The Prince said of another "fallen" woman whom he helped before he came to St. Petersburg:

> I was very sorry for her...I had never, from the very beginning, thought of her as guilty, but only as a poor, unhappy girl. I was very anxious to comfort her and to assure her that there was no reason why she should consider herself beneath everyone.[3]

Daniel Shaw argues that this is the tragic flaw in the Prince's character. It is fine, he says, for the Prince to be truthful, humble and caring; but to carry compassion so far that he won't condemn anyone for past mistakes makes him fall short of being an ideal self, since it conflicts with Dostoevsky's view that we are responsible for our actions:

> [The Prince], due to his all-forgiving nature, did not hold his associates responsible for their actions. It is in this failure that [he] falls very short of the ideal of the God made flesh, and in this falling short reveals his tragic flaw. He treated his fellows as if they were totally determined, and hence couldn't be blamed for their shortcomings.[4]

Although it is certainly true that the Prince's compassion leads to the tragedy at the end of the story, I disagree that Dostoevsky would have us see this as a flaw in his character. Dostoevsky believes both

---

[1] Wasiolek, *Op. Cit.*, p. 104.

[2] *The Idiot*, pp. 76-7.

[3] *Ibid.*, p. 67.

[4] Daniel Shaw, "The Survival of Tragedy: Dostoevsky's 'The Idiot'," *Dialogue*, Vol. 16, 1973, p.11.

that: (1) As free agents, we are responsible for our actions, and (2) individuals should not condemn others, but treat them instead with compassion. These two views are compatible. Dostoevsky maintains that only God, and we ourselves, ought to pass judgment on our behavior. (We should note that the Prince is hard on himself, even though he is compassionate towards others.) We should not pass judgment on others because (a) it is not our place to do so, (b) we are most likely no better than the others we condemn, and (c) it would be counterproductive to do so. People will only improve their behavior through a change of heart coming from within themselves. Blaming others challenges their pride, causing them to want to return the harm they feel has been done to them, and so they become worse, rather than better, persons.

Besides emphasizing compassion, Dostoevsky recommends that we perform "individual acts of charity" as a more productive way of influencing others, rather than blaming them:

> How can you tell what seed may have been dropped in [a person's] soul for ever [through an individual act of charity]....what significance this contact of one personality with another will have for the future of one of them?...In scattering your seed, in offering your 'alms', in doing your good deed, in whatever shape or form, you are giving away part of your personality and absorbing part of another's; you are mutually united to one another....all your scattered seeds, which perhaps you have already forgotten, will take root and grow up; the man who received them from you, will pass them on to someone else. And how can you tell what your contribution to the shaping of man's destinies will be?[1]

There is another potential problem of consistency in Dostoevsky's philosophy, raised by *The Idiot*, which should be mentioned. Does the possibility of an ideal person, represented by the Prince, refute Dostoevsky's view that persons are naturally complex, at least double?

---

[1] *The Idiot*, p. 388. It is interesting to note that it is Ippolit, not the Prince, who says this. Dostoevsky believes that being on the verge of death, which Ippolit is, gives one wisdom. Along these lines, it should be mentioned that the Prince, like Dostoevsky himself, suffered from epilepsy and just before he had a fit, which is much like a little death, he experienced "an intense heightening of awareness."

No. Dostoevsky still maintains that we all have good and evil impulses within us. In this work, though, he emphasizes his belief that we *can* overcome our evil impulses by choosing to act only on our good ones. Even the Prince admits, when listening to a man's confession of having had both "honorable" and "mean" thoughts simultaneously:

> Two ideas occurred to you at one and the same time. This happens very often. It always happens to me. Still, I don't think it's a good thing....it is terribly difficult to fight against these *double* thoughts....The best thing is to leave it to your own conscience, don't you think?[1]

The last part of this quotation is particularly important. How people behave must be left up to individuals' own consciences, because they are free beings. (This is the basis for Dostoevsky's continual rejection of large-scale "social" solutions to the problem of our inability to get along with one another.) The best we can do is try to show others the way to living a good life. One man alone probably cannot make much of a dent in changing the behavior of those used to living in a society where money rules, people are anxious to impress others, maintain their pride, and only think about their own "rights"[2] rather than reaching out to others. Thus the Prince ultimately failed in his mission to help others:

> The Prince is a failure as Christ was a failure, helpless to check the hurt that we do to each other, but ready to take it upon himself and by his own faith to give to all an image of the best of themselves....The Prince cannot change the universe, but a universe of Myshkins might.[3]

Still, the Prince did cause those he came in contact with to pause for a bit and reflect on their destructive behavior. Who knows what seeds he might have sown in them for the future, and what seeds Dostoevsky has undoubtedly sown in his readers in attempting to portray his ideal person. As Dostoevsky said, in characterizing the Russian people, in his *Diary of a Writer*:

---

[1] *The Idiot*, pp. 298-9.

[2] See pp. 192, 247, and pp. 282-3 for a critique of the view that people can achieve happiness by focusing on their rights.

[3] Wasiolek, *Op. Cit.*, p. 109.

[T]he people are not composed of scoundrels only; there are also genuine saints — and what saints! They themselves are radiant and they illuminate the path for all of us![1]

In *The Idiot*, Dostoevsky tried to present us with an ideal of how we ought to behave. In *The Devils*, we are given the opposite: examples of the worst ways that we can use our freedom. Several characters in this novel espouse, and act on, truly frightening beliefs, leaving numerous dead bodies in their wake. Raskolnikov's views and crime pale next to the shocking thoughts and behavior of the "devils" whom Dostoevsky feared most: possible human beings who "lose their way" in life and let the worst side of their natures dominate.

Dostoevsky was particularly concerned about the dangerous time in which he lived: "There are historical moments in the life of men when flagrant, impudent and the coarsest villainy may be deemed a grandeur of the soul...."[2] One of the central events in *The Devils* was based on an actual crime in the news, and the novel contains a number of satirical portraits of Dostoevsky's contemporaries, as well as caricatures of certain types of people of his day. Since we are interested only in Dostoevsky's philosophy, we shall not concern ourselves with the historical aspects of the novel. Instead, we shall focus on the views of the "devils," how they came to acquire them, and how two of them were reformed, at least for a brief time.

The novel takes place in the small town where Stepan Trofimovich Verkhovensky, a once greatly esteemed liberal of the eighteen-forties, has been reduced to living off the charity of Varvara Petrovna Stavrogin, the most socially prominent person in the town. Their not entirely harmonious relationship, resting on undeclared love, began twenty years earlier when Stepan Verkhovensky was hired to be the tutor of Nicholas Stavrogin, Mrs. Stavrogin's son. One of the two most frightening devils in the novel is Nicholas Stavrogin. The other is Stepan Verkhovensky's son from an earlier marriage, Peter, whom he has only seen twice before he makes his appearance in the story.

It seems clear that Dostoevsky believes that the nihilism which infects both Stavrogin and Peter Verkhovensky, and leads to their abominable behavior, is supposed to be traced to Stepan Verkhovensky's liberalism. Stepan Verkhovensky taught the one and

---

[1] *The Diary of a Writer*, 1876, *Op. Cit.*, p. 202.
[2] *Ibid.*, 1873, p. 151.

sired the other. At one point Stepan Verkhovensky says of the sort of socialist views to which both sons have been attracted:

> It's just our idea — yes, ours! We were the first to plant it, to nurture it....But, good Lord, how they have expressed it all, distorted, mutilated it!...Were those the conclusions we wanted to draw? Who can recognize the original idea here?[1]

Stepan Verkhovensky's liberal views are purely intellectual. He enjoys presenting them in witty drawing room discussions, in language liberally sprinkled with French phrases. He has no intention of *acting* on them. He is totally out of touch with reality and rather careless with people. He once lost one of his serfs in a game of cards, leading that man into a life of crime. Stepan Verkhovensky (and others of his kind) bears responsibility for unleashing the devils on the town. For this, we can consider him a minor devil in the story.

Stavrogin is the most enigmatic character in the novel. We are told that "Mr. Verkhovensky succeeded in touching some of the deepest chords in [young Nicholas's] heart," instilling in him a sense of "eternal and sacred longing." Yet after he finished his studies in St. Petersburg, he "gave himself up to a life of mad dissipation," and engaged in "brutal conduct," even in raping a young girl.[2] When he returned home for a time he shocked people with bizarre behavior, like biting the Governor's ear, and yet he fascinated them at the same time, partly because of his physical appearance. He is described as "a paragon of beauty, yet at the same time there was something hideous about him" because "his face reminded them of a mask."

Stavrogin had been traveling for over three years just before he makes his entrance at a gathering in his mother's home. Others who are there include: the Verhovenskys, father and son, who had just been reunited: Mrs. Drozdov, a society matron, and her daughter Lisa; Captain Lebyatkin, a drunken buffoon, and his crippled, half-wit sister Mary; Dasha Shatov, a protégé of Mrs. Stavrogin's, and her brother Ivan, who were formerly Mrs. Stavrogin's serfs. Shortly after Stavrogin's entrance, Ivan Shatov slaps him hard in the face and

---

[1] *The Devils*, p. 308.

[2] According to a chapter of the novel, "Stavrogin's Confession," which the editor of the *Russian Messenger*, where *The Devils* was initially serialized, refused to publish. Dostoevsky chose not to put the chapter back into the novel in subsequent editions.

Stavrogin manages to control his natural reaction to lash back. It becomes, for him, a test of will. He is able to control his feelings.

We learn that Shatov has plenty of reasons to slap him. Stavrogin had an affair with Shatov's wife, who left him a few weeks after their marriage. It is also rumored that he has had a relationship with Shatov's sister; and he married Mary Lebyatkin four years before, "just because of the infamy and absurdity of such a marriage," and then abandoned her. All of this has occurred even though he is unofficially engaged to Lisa Drozdov.

But Shatov didn't slap Stavrogin for any of these reasons. He slapped him "because of [his] fall" from the pedestal Shatov has put him on. Stavrogin once meant a great deal to Shatov. He taught him the philosophy which Shatov has come to believe in passionately, while Stavrogin apparently only briefly flirted with it, just as they both once flirted with Socialism. According to this philosophy, reason and science cannot separate good from evil, and so they have never played more than a secondary role in people's lives. What's really important to people is "the pursuit of God," which is the "spirit of life," the "personality of the people" and its "conception of good and evil." Shatov has added the ideas that each country has its own god, but only one is the true God and this is the God of the Russian people. Shatov is as critical of others' religions — in particular Roman Catholicism which he claims tries to make a god of the State — as he is of Socialism — which denies God in its attempt to organize society entirely on principles of science and reason.

Dostoevsky has put his own views into Shatov's mouth and his murder by Peter Verkhovensky, the leader of a revolutionary socialist group which Shatov has broken with, is the most evil action and the great tragedy of the novel. The murder is so evil because, although it is officially sanctioned on the grounds that Shatov "knows too much" and "might inform the authorities," in fact Peter Verkhovensky has a much more sinister reason for killing him. He has all the members of the group assist him in the murder, and it could have been the murder of anyone, because in this way he can "tie them all up in one knot by the blood they've shed" and then "they'll be [his] slaves."

The tragedy of Shatov's murder lies in the timing. Shatov's only stumbling block to fully accepting his own philosophy is that he doesn't believe in God himself. When Stavrogin asks him whether he believes in God, he splutters:

'I believe in Russia. I believe in the Greek Orthodox Church. I — I believe in the body of Christ — I believe that the second coming will take place in Russia — I believe —' Shatov murmured in a frenzy.

'But in God? In God?'

'I — I shall believe in God.'[1]

Shatov had hoped that Stavrogin would lead him across this final impass — "you alone could have raised the banner!" But Stavrogin let him down. Instead, it takes the twin miracles of the return of Shatov's wife and her giving birth to Stavrogin's child, to enable him to fully embrace life and, we infer, at last believe in God. Sadly, immediately after this occurs, he loses his life.

Stavrogin has also inspired another character's view of life, and it is a much more disturbing view. This character is Kirilov, a structural engineer, who has recently arrived in town and who is known to most of the other characters. He lives in the same complex as Shatov, and they once went to the United States together to learn about the terrible working conditions there first-hand, but they have become estranged since then. Kirilov is concerned with *freedom*, as is his teacher Stavrogin. According to Kirilov: "Full freedom will come only when it makes no difference whether to live or not to live. That's the goal for everybody."[2] There is no God, according to Kirilov. People invent God to cope with pain and fear. "He who conquers pain and fear will himself become a god." He plans to kill himself to show that he has conquered pain and fear, that he has attained ultimate freedom and become god himself. "I am killing myself to show...my new terrible freedom."[3] He hopes that this will usher in a new age for mankind.

But Kirilov, like so many of Dostoevsky's characters, is conflicted. Even as he plans his death, we see that he loves life and children in particular. When Stavrogin points out the inconsistency, he says, "What about it? Why put the two together? Life's one thing, and that's another." Kirilov also believes that "All's good — all. It's good for all those who know that all is good," even "the man who dies of hunger or the man who insults and rapes [a] little girl"[4] is good for the person who believes that all is good.

---

[1] *The Devils*, p. 259.

[2] *Ibid.*, p. 125.

[3] *Ibid.*, p. 615.

[4] The latter is a clear reference to Stavrogin.

Intellectually at least, Kirilov seems to have taken the idea of human freedom to the highest degree. We have no limits on us. There is no God to rein us in and we can choose to believe that the most heinous actions are good, if we wish.[1] Even though Kirilov's philosophy is abhorrent to Dostoevsky, he still presents this character sympathetically. Kirilov has become possessed by an idea, but there is a better side of his nature which expresses itself in his behavior towards others. Although he does succeed in killing himself because of his idea, before that moment he is moved by the plight of others and does all he can to help them. Kirilov's problem, according to Dostoevsky, is that he thinks too much, rather than trusting and acting on his feelings.

More disturbing is Stavrogin, who really lives according to Kirilov's basic philosophy. Stavrogin has been able to conquer not only fear and pain,[2] but *all* human feelings. He is no longer a human being, but rather just a shell of a person, a "mask." He feels no remorse as wreaks havoc with others lives: he is responsible for the deaths of his wife and her brother and ruins Lisa's life, also leading to her death. His only saving grace is that he knows that he is missing something in his life. It is Kirilov who recognizes what ails Stavrogin. He is "looking for a burden," that is, something to which he can commit himself. He realizes that freedom without commitment to something means nothing, as Sartre would later say. Stavrogin can inspire *others* to act, to make commitments — Shatov, Kirilov, Peter Verkhovensky, Lisa, who ruins herself for one night of loving him, and Dasha, who has decided to devote her life to "being there for him," whenever he might need her — yet *he* can't find anything to live for. In the end, he kills himself.

Another person, besides Shatov and Kirilov, whom Stavrogin inspires is Peter Verkhovensky. Peter admits to Stavrogin that "You're my idol!" Why? He says:

---

[1] This appears to be similar to Nietzsche's view of the Overman; but unlike Kirilov's "man-God," who rejects God and suppresses all his desires in order to achieve perfect, but empty, freedom, Nietzsche's Overman becomes a god as a result of having an overflowing, powerful personality and the capability of being his own lawgiver. Nietzsche's Overman would not try to suppress his desires, which are the source of his strength and which he sees as good.

[2] We are told that "Stavrogin was one of those men who knew not the meaning of fear" (*The Devils*, p. 211); and Shatov asks him, "Is it true that the Marquis de Sade could have taken lessons from you?" (p. 260)

Stavrogin, you're beautiful!...you look on everyone as your equal, and everyone is afraid of you. That's good....You're an awful aristocrat. An aristocrat who goes in for democracy is irresistible. To sacrifice life — yours and another man's is nothing to you. You're just the sort of man we need.[1]

It turns out that what Peter Verkhovensky really wants is *power*. He is not really committed to the ideals of Socialism at all. Stavrogin perceptively realizes, "My dear Verhovensky...You're not a socialist at all, it seems, but some sort of — ambitious politician, aren't you?"[2] Peter has accepted the theory of another minor devil in the novel, Shigalyov, a member of the revolutionary group, that the only way to create a harmonious society is that "one-tenth is to be granted absolute freedom and unrestrained powers over the remaining nine-tenths."[3] Those remaining nine-tenths of humanity will not even be considered to be fully human beings for they "must give up their individuality and be turned into something like a herd." Shigalyov admits that "starting from unlimited freedom, I arrived at unlimited despotism."[4] Peter Verkhovensky, of course, sees himself as one of the one-tenth who will rule the others — "slaves must have rulers" — but he realizes that he does not have the charisma to be the supreme leader of the society. This is the role he sees for Stavrogin, a "magnificent and despotic will, an idol of the people."

Peter Verkhovensky has figured out how to bring about Shigalyov's ideal:

> [W]e'll create political disturbances....We shall create such an upheaval that the foundations of the State will be cracked wide open....Every mangy little group will be useful. I'll find you such keen fellows in each one of these groups that they'll be glad to do some shooting and will be grateful for the honour....one or two generations of vice are absolutely essential now. Monstrous, disgusting vice which turns man into an abject, cowardly, and selfish wretch — that's what we want![5]

---

[1] *The Devils*, p. 420.
[2] *Ibid.*, p. 422.
[3] *Ibid.*, p. 405.
[4] *Ibid.*, p. 404.
[5] *Ibid.*, pp. 417-422

At this point everyone in the herd will be equally wretched. "[T]he earth will weep for its old gods" and be ready for a new one to take their place: Stavrogin. Stavrogin is perfect for the job because he has no conscience. He, like Peter, is a nihilist, he's afraid of nothing, he has no aims of his own (so he can be used by the Peter Verkhovenskys of the world), he's aristocratic, he's charismatic and he's mysterious. A legend can be created around him. Peter tells Stavrogin:

> [Y]ou are beautiful, you are proud as a god, you are seeking nothing for yourself, you are "in hiding" with the halo of victim round your head. The main thing is the legend! You will conquer them. You have only to look and you will conquer them.[1]

This is Peter Verkhovensky's dream, but Stavrogin won't cooperate. Even Peter's threats won't work — "understand that you've run up too big an account, and that I can't give you up now" — just because Stavrogin is "afraid of nothing."

Dostoevsky has shown us, in *The Devils*, what he fears most: the worst ways he can think of that people might use their freedom. One can use it to extinguish all of one's natural human feelings in order to achieve maximal freedom (one will no longer be "controlled" by desires), in the process destroying all that is good in oneself and one's ability to distinguish good from evil, and then be unable to find anything to live for, as Stavrogin does. Stavrogin acts on the views expressed by Kirilov, who is not really able to live in accordance with his own ideal. Or one could use one's freedom to gain power over others at any cost, ignoring all those who are hurt in the process, as Peter Verkhovensky does, putting Shigalyov's theory into practice. What the two abuses of one's freedom have in common is the rejection of absolute values and God, so that one can become a god oneself. Both Stavrogin and Peter Verkhovensky are nihilists[2] and atheists. In the next novel, Dostoevsky's magnum opus *The Brothers Karamazov*, he will argue that we must use our freedom to believe in God in order to escape nihilism and its destructive consequences — madness, suicide and the permissibility of destroying others.

---

[1] *The Devils*, p. 423.

[2] Stavrogin says, in the removed "Confession," that "I neither know nor feel good or evil...[which] is just a prejudice." (*The Devils*, p. 692)

Only Shatov, for a brief moment before his death, and Stepan Verkhovensky, at the end of the novel, point the way toward salvation. Dostoevsky has Stepan Verkhovensky pay a penance at the end, for unwittingly unleashing the devils on the town of Skvoreshniki: "for twenty years you've been forcing all the ideas that have now come to a head on people — the fruits of your teaching we're gathering now."[1] He sets out on a pilgrimage, a knight on a quest, to discover the heart of Russia in the peasants with whom he has never been in touch. He finds God through a peasant woman who is selling copies of the Gospel. He discovers that nothing is "more precious than love," that we must "forgive all" because "all, every one of us, have wronged one another. We are all guilty!", that "Every minute, every second of life ought to be a blessing to man....It is the duty of every man to make it so." Finally, he learns that "If God exists [and he does], then [we are] immortal." We can feel better about the sad fates of Shatov and Stepan Verkhovensky, who also dies at the end, since they have only left this earthly existence.

Stepan Verkhovensky even anticipates his own and others' deaths, maintaining that they are deserved, and that all will turn out for the best. Applying a story from Luke in the Bible[2] about the devils who went out of a madman and entered into swine who threw themselves off a cliff into the sea and drown, thus saving the man, he says:

> [The swine] are we, we and them, and Peter — *et les autre avec lui*, and perhaps I at the head of them all, and we shall cast ourselves down, the raving and the possessed, from the cliff into the sea and shall all be drowned, and serves us right, for that is all we are good for. But the sick man [that is, Russia] will be healed, and "will sit at the feet of Jesus", and all will look at him and be amazed.[3]

---

[1] Governor Lembke to Stepan Verkhovensky, *The Devils*, p. 447.
[2] This was the prefatory quotation with which *The Devils* began.
[3] *The Devils*, p. 648.

6

The Brothers Karamazov

"You have not made up your mind what answer to give to [the God and immortality] question and therein lies your great grief, for the question urgently demands an answer....If you can't answer it in the affirmative, you will never be able to answer it in the negative. You know that peculiarity of your heart yourself — and all its agony is due to that alone." (the elder Father Zossima to Ivan, *The Brothers Karamazov*[1])

"God and the devil are fighting for mastery, and the battlefield is the heart of man." (Dmitry to Alyosha, *The Brothers Karamazov*[2])

Dostoevsky's philosophy is most fully expressed in *The Brothers Karamazov*, a huge novel which, like *Crime and Punishment*, is centered around the events leading up to, and the aftermath of, a murder. In this case it is Fyodor Karamazov, the father of three legitimate sons — and, it is rumored, one illegitimate son — who is killed. Fyodor Karamazov is described as being a "muddle-headed and

---

[1] *The Brothers Karamazov*, translated by David Magarshack, Penguin Books, New York, 1982, p. 78.
[2] *Ibid.*, p. 124.

preposterous fellow" who has a special knack for making money. Physically, he is repulsive:

> In addition to the long fleshy bags under his little eyes, which were always insolent, suspicious, and sardonic, in addition to the multitude of deep wrinkles on his fat little face, there hung under his sharp chin a large Adam's apple, fleshy and longish like a little purse, which gave him a sort of revolting sensual appearance. Add to that a long, cruel, and sensual mouth with full lips, between which could be seen stumps of black and almost decayed teeth. He sputtered every time he began to speak.[1]

Two of the legitimate sons, Dmitry and Ivan, hate their father and could have been responsible for his death. Dmitry (also called Mitya), the oldest son, is impulsive, passionate, and has been known to have acted violently in the past. He and his father are both vying for the attention of the same "fallen woman," Grushenka, even though Dmitry is engaged to another woman, Katerina. Furthermore, Dmitry believes that his father has not given him the full inheritance he is due from his deceased mother. Ivan, Fyodor Karamazov's son from a second marriage, is an intellectual who appears to have no moral scruples to prevent him from acting on his feelings of repugnance towards his father. He does not believe in God and has put forth the theory that, without a belief in God and immortality, "there would be nothing immoral then, everything would be permitted, even cannibalism."[2]

Only the third legitimate son, Alexey (also called Alyosha), who is also the product of Fyodor Karamazov's second marriage, does not hate his father. Indeed, this gentle young man, who initially appears in the novel as a novice who has spent the last year in a monastery not far from the Karamazov estate, bears no ill-will towards anyone. He is described as being much like Prince Myshkin in *The Idiot*, except that he is a "realist":

> [He] loved people: all his life he seemed to have complete faith in people, and yet no one ever took him for a simpleton or a naive person....he did not want to set himself up as a

---

[1] *The Brothers Karamazov*, p. 23.

[2] *Ibid.*, p. 77.

judge of people....he tolerated everything without in the least passing judgment, though often grieving bitterly.[1]

Alyosha spends much of his time desperately trying to keep the peace and preventing the other characters from doing something they will regret. Inspired by his hero, the elder Father Zossima, Alyosha dreams of a time when:

> [A]ll will be holy, and will love each other, and there will be no more rich nor poor, exalted nor humbled, but all men will be as the children of God and the real kingdom of Christ will come.[2]

The illegitimate son, Smerdyakov, is treated as a servant in Fyodor Karamazov's household. His mother was a local idiot whom drinking companions once dared Fyodor Karamazov to "regard as a woman." Smerdyakov is an epileptic who is described as having "a supercilious character" and as "seem[ing] to despise everyone." It turns out that he is the one who committed the murder, feigning an epileptic fit to serve as his alibi. He admired Ivan and believed that this is what Ivan wished him to do.

Dmitry is observed at the scene of the crime. He is arrested and eventually convicted, largely on the basis of evidence given by his spurned fiancé Katerina, whose pride has been injured. When Ivan learns of the part he played in motivating the murder, he loses his mind. Even when he confesses, in an attempt to help his brother, no one believes him. Smerdyakov ends up hanging himself.

Early in the novel, Father Zossima "went down on his knees" before Dmitry, sensing that he had much suffering in store for him. Dmitry, for a time, is willing to accept his punishment because he had desired his father's death: "I accept my punishment not because I killed him, but because I wanted to kill him and, perhaps, would, in fact, have killed him."[3] He feels reborn through his ordeal:

> I've felt the presence of a new man in me....He was shut up inside me, but he would never have appeared, had it not been for this bolt from the blue!....And there seems to be so much

---

[1] *The Brothers Karamazov*, p. 18.
[2] *Ibid.*, p. 32.
[3] *Ibid.*, p. 598.

strength in me now that I shall overcome all things, all suffering.[1]

He has been saved by love, for Grushenka has at last committed to him: "I've taken all her soul into my soul and through her I've become a man myself!"[2] Later, he is happy that Ivan planned a way for him to escape before he went completely insane because he knows that they won't allow convicts to marry.

The Brothers Karamazov ends with a scene at the graveside of Ilyusha, a brave little boy who tragically died not long after Dmitry offended his father. In words reminiscent of Ippolit's idea, presented in *The Idiot*, of the importance of positively affecting people's lives by planting "seeds" in them, Alyosha tells a group of young boys:

> [L]et us never forget how happy we were here, when we were all of us together, united by such a good and kind feeling, which made us, too, while we loved the poor little boy, better men, perhaps, than we are....there's nothing higher, stronger, more wholesome and more useful in life than some good memory....even if only one good memory is left in our hearts, it may also be the instrument of our salvation one day.[3]

In this last novel, we are finally given complete answers to the two basic philosophical questions which Dostoevsky has only partially answered in earlier novels: (i) What is the human predicament? and (ii) How should we live our lives? Dostoevsky's view of the human predicament can be summarized in five claims that he makes: (1) "[A]ll but man is perfect and without sin...."[4] (2) Human beings have free will in the libertarian sense. This is their dearest possession. (3) Adult human beings are complex, having conflicting impulses within them: "we possess broad, unrestrained natures...capable of accommodating all sorts of extremes...."[5] (4) Some of these impulses incline adults to sin: "In every man...a wild beast is hidden."[6] (5) Children, however, are without sin: "children..., like the angels, are without sin, and live to

[1] *The Brothers Karamazov*, pp. 694-5.
[2] *Ibid.*, p. 698.
[3] *Ibid.*, p. 910-11.
[4] *Ibid.*, p. 346.
[5] *Ibid.*, p. 824.
[6] *Ibid.*, p. 283.

arouse tender feelings in us and to purify our hearts, and are a sort of guidance to us."[1]

Let us reflect on each of these claims. From the first, we learn that Dostoevsky does not recognize the existence of what philosophers have called "natural" or "physical" evil, that is evil which is not caused by human beings. Usually philosophers divide the evil which exists in the universe into two types: (a) "man-made" or "moral" evil and (b) "natural" or "physical" evil. The first category would include such actions as murder and torture; the second would include diseases and natural disasters. Doesn't Dostoevsky consider cancer and a tornado, which cause much suffering, to be evil? Apparently not. It's hard to defend the idea that "all but man is perfect," given the existence of diseases, which ravage the mind and body, and natural disasters, which destroy lives; but Dostoevsky could maintain they are "without sin" on the grounds that they do not involve the *intentional* infliction of suffering. However, if we assume that there is an all-powerful and all-knowing God who created the universe, then it would appear that He causes or permits these events to occur. This would mean that examples of natural evil also involve the intentional infliction of suffering on individuals.

The remaining four claims have been introduced in earlier Dostoevsky novels. We have seen how important human freedom is to Dostoevsky and also how concerned he is about how it might be abused. Dostoevsky has consistently maintained that human beings have good and bad impulses within them, and that acting on the latter impulses can lead to much harm. In this final novel, Dostoevsky has a more developed view of the complexity of adult human beings, of what in us can cause us to go astray and also what enables us to act properly. We see, in the three legitimate Karamazov sons, exaggerations of three components of the human personality, as Dostoevsky now pictures it: the sensual, the intellectual and the spiritual components. In Dmitry, the sensual aspect is dominant; in Ivan, the intellectual part dominates; and in Alyosha, it is the spiritual part which is predominant.[2]

It is important to note that in each man all three components exist; but by having exaggerations of the three components in three different individuals, Dostoevsky is able to show us the strengths and

[1] *The Brothers Karamazov*, pp. 375-6.
[2] The illegitimate son Smerdyakov, who admired Ivan, seems to represent the perversion of reason. See, for example, his bizarre arguments on pp. 148-153.

weaknesses of each of the three parts of the human personality. We see that sensual excesses can lead to sin, that the intellect can torment an individual[1] and lead to the development of theories which support the abuse of human beings (reinforcing lessons we learned in *Crime and Punishment* and *The Devils*), and that the spiritual aspect of the human being is the best part.

The last of the five claims Dostoevsky makes about the human predicament — that children are without sin — raises an interesting problem: How do children, who are without sin, become adults, who generally are sinners? Do the three parts of the adult human personality, two of which can lead people to sin, take time to develop in human beings? Or do adults corrupt children at a certain stage in their development?

How should we live our lives, according to Dostoevsky? A few preliminaries must be stated. Dostoevsky believes that: (6) We are responsible for our own actions (given 2). (7) A universal moral code is dependent upon a belief in God and immortality. Dostoevsky is convinced that only God could give the authority to support an absolute moral code, and the promise of immortality allows virtue to be rewarded eventually, even though it may not be in this life. Without the belief in God and immortality "everything would be permitted."

Dostoevsky, it would appear, accepts the reasoning behind Kant's famous "moral argument" for the existence of God: We must be moral, but realistically we know that our good behavior will not necessarily be rewarded in this life. In order for our being moral to make sense, there must be an eventual uniting of virtue and happiness: the *summum bonum*. There must, therefore, be a God and an afterlife in which God rewards or punishes us according to our behavior in this life. In disagreement with Kant and other philosophers, however, Dostoevsky maintains that: (8) The intellect cannot give us a reason for living. One is lost if one succumbs to the sterile intellect. As Alyosha tells Ivan, the character in whom the intellectual aspect of the personality dominates: "Love life...regardless of logic....Yes, most certainly regardless of logic, for only then will [one] grasp its meaning."[2] Dostoevsky would not fully accept Kant's moral argument, because Kant's argument ultimately rests on the idea that the principle of morality — Kant's Categorical Imperative — is the only *rational* principle one could adopt. For Kant, we must be moral because it's rational. This is not true

---

[1] Ivan is driven insane and Smerdyakov hangs himself.

[2] *The Brothers Karamazov*, p. 269.

for Dostoevsky, for whom the impulse to be moral comes from the spiritual aspect of the person, not the intellect.

From (7) and (8), Dostoevsky concludes that any attempts to give meaning to life (and solve problems like the social organization of mankind) which are founded on reason (the intellect), and reject the existence of God, are doomed. Dostoevsky particularly attacks the intellectual theory of Socialism. And given (2) and (6), Dostoevsky rejects any religious institution which deprives human beings of their free will and moral responsibility for their actions. This is the basis for Dostoevsky's attack on Roman Catholicism, as we shall see.

It is very important to Dostoevsky that we use our freedom correctly. Dostoevsky concludes that to find meaning in life and support for an absolute moral code which respects other human beings: (9) We must freely turn to God, surrendering to the love of God, and (10) become more Christ-like ourselves through the "active love" of others.[1] The elder Father Zossima and Alyosha — the two characters in whom the spiritual part of the personality dominates — flesh out the particulars of how we ought to behave. We should: (a) avoid becoming isolated from others, but instead (b) love other human beings, particularly those who sin most, since they most need our love,[2] (c) feel responsible for every other person, since we have the ability to positively affect others' lives, (d) be humble, for we are no better than anyone else, (e) not judge others,[3] only ourselves, and (f) be truthful.[4]

Finally, given (1), Dostoevsky says that: (11) we should love the earth and all that is in nature. In a moment of ecstasy for Alyosha, "the mystery of the earth came in contact with the mystery of the [heavens]." He "threw himself down flat upon the earth" and "vowed frenziedly to love it, to love it forever and ever."[5]

---

[1] For Dostoevsky, losing the ability to love is the worst thing that could happen to a person: "What is hell?...The suffering that comes from the consciousness that one is no longer able to love." (pp. 379-80)

[2] "Everything can be atoned for, everything can be saved by love." (p. 56)

[3] For people's behavior to be improved "it is necessary that men themselves should suffer a change of heart." (p. 356)

[4] One who continually lies "gets to a point where he can't distinguish any truth in himself or in those around him, and so he loses all respect for himself and for others. Having no respect for anyone, he ceases to love...." (p. 47)

[5] *The Brothers Karamazov*, p. 426.

The ideal we should be striving for in our relations with others is society's taking on the character of "a single, universal, and sovereign church," the state having withered away. Dostoevsky envisions the possibility of our attaining a type of existence which one could describe as "heaven" on earth, if we all were to simultaneously freely accept God and actively love one another. Unlike a society governed by an atheistic State, which can deprive individuals of their freedom and can justify doing anything in the name of the State's interest, Dostoevsky's ideal society would respect human beings' freedom and rest on absolute values which acknowledge the value of each human being.

It is very important for Dostoevsky that we *freely* choose to accept God. Thus, he maintains that miracles should not play a part in acquiring or maintaining faith. Miracles take away uncertainty about God's existence. We would *have* to believe in God, if miracles occurred, rather than leaving it up to the individual's free will whether or not to believe in God.[1] For the same reason, Dostoevsky claims that one cannot prove God's existence or understand His ways.

The greatest obstacle to accepting the existence of God is the Problem of Evil: the problem of reconciling the existence of a benevolent (all-good), omniscient (all-knowing) and omnipotent (all-powerful) creator of the universe, given the evil which exists in the world. God must know that the evil occurs, since He is omniscient; He must want to eliminate it, since He is benevolent; and He is able to eliminate it, since He is omnipotent. So why does evil exist? It would appear that since evil exists, God cannot.

Dostoevsky wrestles with this problem in what is probably the finest two chapters in all of his novels: the chapters "Rebellion" and "The Grand Inquisitor" of *The Brothers Karamazov*. In these chapters we see Ivan's mind at work, a mind which its owner admitted in the chapter before is "a Euclidean, an earthly mind," one which is unable "to solve problems which are not of this world." This means that Ivan approaches the problem rationally. He needs a logical solution to the problem of evil in order to accept the existence of God.

In "Rebellion," Ivan lays out the problem to Alyosha in such a way that it would appear to be rationally unsolvable. He decides to focus on adults' brutal treatment of children, which is certainly the most disturbing part of the problem of evil. How could a benevolent,

---

[1] "[F]aith does not arise from a miracle, but the miracle from faith." (p. 26)

omnipotent, omniscient God allow this to occur? Dostoevsky invites us to suffer along with Alyosha, as he vividly presents us with real-life examples of terrible things that have been done by adult human beings to children. As Ivan says, although "people sometimes speak of man's 'bestial' cruelty," in fact "a beast can never be so cruel as a man, so ingeniously, so artistically cruel":

> [O]ne incident I found particularly interesting. Imagine a baby in the arms of a trembling mother, surrounded by Turks who had just entered her house. They are having great fun: they fondle the baby, they laugh to make it laugh and they are successful: the baby laughs. At that moment the Turk points a pistol four inches from the baby's face. The boy laughs happily, stretches out his little hands to grab the pistol, when suddenly the artist pulls the trigger in the baby's face and blows his brains out.[1]

He tells us, also, about a five year old girl who was repeatedly beaten and tortured by her parents and then shut up in a cold outhouse all night after her mother made her eat her own excrement when she soiled herself. And he tells us about a General who, upset because an eight year old serf boy accidentally hurt the paw of his favorite hound in play, had the boy "stripped naked" and commanded him to run while an entire pack of hounds hunted him down and "tore him to pieces."

What bothers Ivan is the *innocence* of the children. He can understand why adults who have sinned might have to suffer, "but then there are the children, and what am I to do with them?" "It is entirely incomprehensible why they, too, should have to suffer," according to Ivan. It is unjust to have them suffer for the sins of others. Furthermore, one cannot say it is all right that they suffer because "a child is bound to grow up and sin" since, in the case of the serf boy, "he didn't grow up; he was torn to pieces by dogs at the age of eight."

If the suffering of innocent children is necessary to achieve some "higher harmony," Ivan says that it is not worth the price. "It is not worth one little tear of that tortured little girl who beat herself on the breast and prayed to her 'dear, kind Lord' in the stinking privy with her unexpiated tears!" The chapter climaxes with Ivan asking Alyosha:

---

[1] *The Brothers Karamazov*, p. 279.

[I]magine that it is you yourself who are erecting the edifice of human destiny with the aim of making men happy in the end, of giving them peace and contentment at last, but that to do that it is absolutely necessary, and indeed quite inevitable, to torture to death only one tiny creature, the little girl who beat her breast with her little fist, and to found the edifice on her unavenged tears — would you consent to be the architect on those conditions?[1]

Even though Alyosha believes in God, he answers "No, I wouldn't." But it's clear that Alyosha is willing to accept that what looks bad from our finite perspective, can be reconciled with the existence of a benevolent, omnipotent and omniscient God. He doesn't expect to understand; but Ivan, the intellectual, must have an answer here and now, and there doesn't seem to be an answer which could satisfy him.

A crucial part of the problem for Ivan lies in his understanding of "benevolence." It would appear that, for Ivan, a truly benevolent being would eliminate suffering, at least the suffering of innocent beings, in so far as he could. Since innocent beings do suffer, according to Ivan there cannot be a benevolent, omniscient, omnipotent God. Later philosophers who have wrestled with the problem of evil have proposed a different definition of benevolence. Perhaps influenced by utilitarian thinking, they have suggested that a benevolent being might bring about the greatest net good, and that this is compatible with there being much evil in the world.[2]

In the story of "The Grand Inquisitor," which immediately follows "Rebellion," Dostoevsky gives his solution to the problem of evil. It is not clear to many readers that Dostoevsky is giving us his solution because he presents it indirectly, that is by showing that the opposite of the view he supports is unacceptable. Ivan tells a tale about Jesus' reappearance on earth, in Spain, "during the most terrible time of the Inquisition" in the Fifteenth Century. The Cardinal, the ancient Grand

---

[1] *The Brothers Karamazov*, p. 287.

[2] The most sophisticated argument to demonstrate the compatibility of the existence of God with considerable evil in the universe was given by Alvin Plantinga. See, for instance, his book *God, Freedom, and Evil* (Harper and Row, New York, 1974). In my article, "Plantinga and the Free Will Defense" (*Pacific Philosophical Quarterly*, vol. 62, no. 3, 1981), I argue that there are many problems with his solution to the problem of evil.

Inquisitor, has been ordering the burning of many heretics at the stake. When the Grand Inquisitor realizes that Jesus has come back to earth, he has his guards arrest Him and he later visits Him in his prison cell.

The Grand Inquisitor tells Jesus that "*he* has no right to add anything to what had already been said before," that everything was handed over to the Pope. The Roman Catholic Church has "corrected" God's work by eliminating the greatest obstacle to the masses of people attaining happiness in this life: *freedom*. As long as human beings are free, the Grand Inquisitor tells Jesus, there will never be enough food for everyone, for "they will never, never be able to let everyone have his fair share." And few people will be strong enough "to give up the earthly bread for the bread of heaven." The vast majority of people who are weak and starving, and find their freedom to be a burden, have gladly handed their freedom over to the Catholic Church on the promise that it will feed them and tell them how they should live. Only the leaders are free. The Church even allows the masses to sin, as long as it is with its "permission". The Catholic Church has corrected God's work by basing its system on "miracle, mystery, and authority" which God had rejected as a basis for faith, since they deprive people of the freedom to believe in God or not. The story ends with Jesus saying nothing to the Grand Inquisitor; instead He "kissed him gently on his bloodless, aged lips." The Grand Inquisitor lets Jesus go. "The kiss glows in his heart, but the old man sticks to his idea."

The Grand Inquisitor has clearly adopted the philosophy of the minor devil Shigalyov in *The Devils*: the only way to achieve a harmonious society is "for one-tenth to be granted absolute freedom and unrestrained powers over the remaining nine-tenths" who will "be turned into something like a herd." The Church is using Religion as its banner, in seizing power over the majority of the people; but even the Grand Inquisitor recognizes that it has rejected God in order to achieve the happiness of the majority. The leaders will keep this knowledge to themselves: "we shall keep the secret and for their own happiness will entice them with the reward of heaven," even though "beyond the grave they will find nothing but death."

As Dostoevsky sees the issue, God was faced with a choice between maximizing human *happiness*, which could only be achieved by depriving human beings of their free will, or allowing them to have *free will*, even though much suffering might result from the choices they make. Dostoevsky, who believes that human beings' freedom is their dearest possession, thinks that God should have, and did, elect the second option. Free will is worth any amount of suffering which is introduced into the world as a result. Dostoevsky is hoping that we will agree with Alyosha who says that Ivan's tale "is in praise of Jesus," even though He says nothing. The Grand Inquisitor refutes his own position. We don't want to be deprived of our freedom, even for happiness.

The other main obstacle, besides the problem of evil, which Dostoevsky acknowledges is a stumbling block to accepting his view of how we ought to live our lives, is the aversion we feel towards particular human beings. Dostoevsky admits that it is easier to love human beings in the abstract than in the flesh. As Ivan says: "I never could understand how one can love one's neighbours. In my view, it is one's neighbours that one can't possibly love, but only perhaps those who live far away."[1] Dmitry, for instance, found it impossible to love his father: "I hate his Adam's apple, his nose, his eyes, his shameless sneer. I feel a physical aversion."[2] Father Zossima tells us that it isn't always easy to love others, that "active love means hard work and tenacity."

Dostoevsky believes that we can't *force* human beings to love one another. It must come from within human beings themselves:

> It's a spiritual, a psychological process. To transform the world, it is necessary that men themselves should suffer a change of heart. Until you have actually become everyone's brother, the brotherhood of man will not come to pass.[3]

Until such time comes that there is an end to the "dreadful isolation of man," Dostoevsky advises:

> [T]ill then we must keep the banner flying and, even if he has to do it alone, a man has to set an example at least once and draw his soul out of isolation and work for some great act of human intercourse based on brotherly love, even if he is to be regarded as a saintly fool for his pains. He has to do so that the great idea may not die.[4]

---

[1] *The Brothers Karamazov*, p. 276.
[2] *Ibid.*, p. 141.
[3] *Ibid.*, p. 356.
[4] *Ibid.*, p. 357.

7

Final Assessment

We are now in a position to give a final assessment of Dostoevsky's philosophy, of the views which evolved as he wrote his great novels and which are most fully and clearly expressed in *The Brothers Karamazov*. Some of these views can be questioned; but his vision of what life could be, if we only use our free will correctly, is certainly one of the most inspiring visions to have ever been given.

Let us begin with Dostoevsky's picture of the human predicament. As I have already indicated, it is problematical that he did not recognize the existence of natural evil, given his belief in God. This is certainly a weakness in his overall philosophical position, but not, I think, devastating. Alvin Plantinga has shown that the free will solution to the problem of man-made evil can be extended to cover natural evil as well, since other beings created by God, "fallen" angels perhaps, might be responsible for this type of evil through the abuse of their freedom.

Dostoevsky's entire philosophy hinges on his belief that we have free will in the libertarian sense. It is controversial whether we have this sort of freedom, and many philosophers question whether it is even intelligible. It is maintained that either an action arises from the self's character being what it is, in which case the action is *determined* by the nature of the self; or else the action is not caused by anything in the self, but just happens "out of the blue," in which case the self is not responsible for it. Although this criticism appears to be devastating to the libertarian conception of freedom, I have argued elsewhere that this conception of freedom is intelligible.[1]

Some would question whether our having free will in the libertarian sense is even compatible with the existence of God. Can we be free in this sense, if there is a God who is omnipotent and omniscient? I think one can maintain that although God *could* stop human beings from acting freely, he chooses not to. In this way God's omnipotence can be preserved. It is more difficult to show the compatibility of God's omniscience with human beings acting freely in the libertarian sense. I would argue that an omniscient being can only know all that it is logically possible to know. It seems to me that future free actions — free in the libertarian sense — are unknowable. Dostoevsky is right, in my opinion, to say that God (assuming He exists) must have decided that free will is worth any amount of evil which might result from this freedom, because even He couldn't know beforehand whether our good actions would outweigh our evil ones.

Dostoevsky's view that adult human beings are complex, having conflicting impulses — some of which can incline them to sin and others to do good actions — seems intuitively correct. His dividing the personality into *three* parts is a view which has been held by Plato and Freud, although they have characterized the three components slightly differently from Dostoevsky's "sensual", "intellectual", and "spiritual" components. We can also appreciate Dostoevsky's view that young children are innocent and in some respects can serve as a sort of guidance to us. It is interesting to note that the highest stage in the development of creativity for the potential overman, according to Nietzsche, is the "child" stage which represents innocence, a forgetting, a new beginning.

As we look at Dostoevsky's preliminary observations concerning how we ought to live our lives, the claim which most philosophers will find shocking is that the rational (intellectual) part of a person is not the best part of us. It can lead us astray. This view can be found in Kierkegaard's and Nietzsche's writings as well.[2] All three emphasize love/passion as the key to making the most of one's life; and as

---

[1] See "The Libertarian Conception of Freedom," *International Philosophical Quarterly*, Vol. XXI, no. 4, 1981.

[2] See Kierkegaard's *Concluding Unscientific Postscript* and Nietzsche's "On the Prejudices of Philosophers" in *Beyond Good and Evil*.

Kierkegaard says, "passion and reflection are generally exclusive of one another."[1]

There is, however, a crucial difference between Dostoevsky and the other two. Dostoevsky is ultimately a collectivist, whereas the other two are individualists. According to Kierkegaard, we are free to choose to live for ourselves (the aesthetic way of life), for others (the ethical way of life), or for God (the religious way of life). Nietzsche recommends the first option for his potential overman and Kierkegaard recommends the third option, which he maintains involves establishing a one-to-one relationship with God. Both involve the individual committing to a way of life which may not be right for others. Dostoevsky, on the other hand, is committed to *the ethical way of life*, and not as one option for how one can live, but as *the only correct way*. And for Dostoevsky, unlike Kierkegaard, the ethical way of life is crucially tied to the religious way of life.[2]

Dostoevsky accepts the existence of absolute values, that is values which we he believes we *all* ought to accept. We are free to reject them; but if we do, we will pay a heavy price. Since, if we reject the existence of absolute values, "everything is permitted," we cannot be surprised if people commit the most atrocious crimes.

Next to his belief that we are free in the libertarian sense, the most crucial assumption in Dostoevsky's overall philosophical position is that only God could provide the support for an absolute code of values. Thus, for him, whether or not there is a God, we need to *believe* that there is one, or else "everything is permitted": "if there were no God, it would have been necessary to invent him....I made up my mind long ago not to speculate whether man has created God or God has created man."[3]

I suggest that the main challenge Dostoevsky poses for philosophers, in particular ethicists, is whether it is possible to find any other support for an absolute code of values than belief in God. Twentieth Century philosophers attempted to pry Ethics away from Religion, but it is not clear that they were successful in discovering another foundation for an absolute code of values. Few ethicists find

---

[1] *Concluding Unscientific Postscript*, in Robert Bretall, *A Kierkegaard Anthology*, Princeton University Press, Princeton, N. J., 1973, p. 255.
[2] The two are not tied together for Kierkegaard because God might ask us, as he did Abraham, to do something unethical as a test of faith.
[3] *The Brothers Karamazov*, p. 274.

Ethical Relativism to be acceptable, but can they support any *absolute* values once the underpinning of Religion has been removed?

A defender of Socialism in *The Brothers Karamazov* challenges Dostoevsky's view with the following words:

> Mankind will find in itself the strength to live for virtue even without believing in [God and] the immortality of the soul! It will find it in love for freedom, equality, fraternity.[1]

But what will the incentive be for caring about equality and fraternity when it isn't in people's self-interest to do so, if people don't believe in God and an afterlife? And what might people do with their freedom if they believe themselves to be "man-gods"[2]? These are the questions Dostoevsky would ask. He would add that even in the name of "freedom, equality and fraternity," they might, and have, killed many people.

Whether we agree with Dostoevsky that Ethics must be based on Religion, or not, certainly his ethical values are very admirable. Dostoevsky gives us his vision of an ideal world which few would doubt is morally superior to the existing world of greed, inequality, envy and bloodshed. He says that in his ideal world there will be:

> universal communion of men...the maintenance of complete liberty of men, with the indication of what liberty comprises, *i.e.*, loving communion, guaranteed by deeds, by the living example, by the factual need of brotherhood, and not under the threat of the guillotine, not by means of chopping off millions of heads....[3]

The tantalizing part of Dostoevsky's philosophy is that if we have the sort of free will he thinks we have, his vision could become a reality. In the meantime, I, for one, am willing to try to actively love others, to plant a "seed" in others and hope it takes root. What do we have to lose? Only our "pride" as we perhaps appear to be "saintly fools."

---

[1] *The Brothers Karamazov*, p. 92.

[2] In an interesting scene in *The Brothers Karamazov*, Ivan confronts his personal devil who reprises the Kirilov view of life from *The Devils*.

[3] *The Diary of a Writer*, 1877, p. 582.

Selected Bibliography

Crime and Punishment, Fyodor Dostoevsky, translated by David McDuff, Penguin Books, New York, 1991.

Dostoevsky, A Biography, Leonid Grossman, translated by Mary Mackler, The Bobbs-Merrill Company, New York, 1975.

Dostoevsky, A Collection of Critical Essays, edited by René Wellek, Prentice-Hall, Englewood Cliffs, New Jersey, 1962.

Dostoevsky, The Major Fiction, Edward Wasiolek, The M.I.T. Press, Cambridge, Mass., 1964.

Feodor Dostoevsky, Alba Amoia, Continuum Publishing Company, New York, 1993.

"Freedom and Love in *Notes from Underground*," Lawrence Stern, Philosophy Research Archives, Vol. 4, 1978.

Freedom and the Tragic Life, A Study in Dostoevsky, Vyacheslav Ivanov, The Noonday Press, New York, 1959.

Fyodor Dostoevsky, A Writer's Life, Geir Kjetsaa, Viking, New York, 1987.

"Nietzsche's 'Discovery' of Dostoevsky," C. A. Miller, *Nietzsche-Studien*, Vol. 2, 1973.

Notes from Underground and The Double, Fyodor Dostoevsky, translated by Jessie Coulson, Penguin Books, New York, 1972.

The Brothers Karamazov, Fyodor Dostoevsky, translated by David Magarshack, Penguin Books, New York, 1982.

The Devils, Fyodor Dostoevsky, translated by David Magarshack, Penguin Books, New York, 1971.

The Diary of a Writer, Fyodor Dostoevsky, translated by Boris Brasol, George Braziller, New York, 1954.

The Idiot, Fyodor Dostoevsky, translated by David Magarshack, Penguin Books, New York, 1955.

"The Survival of Tragedy: Dostoevsky's 'The Idiot'," Daniel Shaw, *Dialogue*, Vol. 16, 1973.